Three Steps to Sustainability: A Practical Guide to Methods and Tools
For Sustainable Project Management

Heinz Fabrinsky

Three Steps to Sustainability:

A Practical Guide to Methods and Tools for Sustainable Project Management

Bibliographical Information of the Deutsche Nationalbibliothek
This publication is listed in the Deutsche Nationalbibliographie of the Deutsche Nationalbibliothek; detailed bibliographical information can be accessed under http: //dnb.d-nb.de

© 2014 Heinz Fabrinsky
Printing, Production and Layout: BoD – Books on Demand
ISBN: 978-3-7357-5531-5

Table of Contents

Preface

This book has been published with support from *BibeZu Bildung für eine bessere Zukunft gemeinnützige GmbH*.

It is an incorporated, certified charitable organization which collects donations and contributions from sponsors, as well as receiving public funding. These means are used to conduct research on sustainable development and various kinds of educational activities on that topic.

Besides that it offers consulting services and tools for sustainable management. Examples are consulting for the *CO_2-free company*, licenses for checklists and other tools, and *prognotherm* (an application for energy management with sustainable sources). Revenues from these products and services contribute to the projects mentioned above.

Thanks to

1. Introduction

1.1 Motivation

Ever since we human beings started to live and work as economic actors we wanted to keep the level of prosperity we achieved and enhance it, whenever possible. As project managers, program managers, and portfolio managers we are always looking for incentives, ideas, tools and methods to improve our businesses and organizations. The current changes in our societies and the creation of new technologies are leading to ever changing markets. Therefore we are constantly looking for ways of creating a competitive edge by adapting to these changes or even better, ways to drive that change.

However it seems that these changes and results of our economic activities do not always contribute to positive developments of society and environment. There are rising concerns about a global climate change induced by burning fossil fuels and releasing carbon dioxide into the atmosphere. Demanding work environments seem to cause rising figures of psychosomatic diseases. Growing concentration of income and disparities in wealth, especially between the northern and southern hemispheres, are causing pressures through illegal migration with all its symptoms in our societies. These effects are also causing higher costs for our companies, as we will see in the following sections, and so putting our current and future profits at risk.

Wouldn't it then be great, if you came up to your senior management with progressive ideas and methods to save money for your organization, enhance perception in the market and set the trends for a prosperous future? These are the effects when we add value to our clients, to our natural and social environment and our organization itself without wasting natural or social resources around us. This was the reason for me to write this book, so that we can better learn how to create these important effects by conducting our projects in a better way.

1.2 Current Problems

1.2.1 Social Topics

In today's economic and political environment we are faced with many phenomena which are sustainably threatening our prosperity. We can start by looking at social topics. There are problems of unemployment, especially in southern Europe, where we find more than 20% of people in Spain or Greece being without a job. Many of the unemployment issues seem to be related to problems of debt overload. High debts means higher interest rates, less investment, more economic uncertainty, instabilities in exchange rates and so on. But where do these high debts come from?

There are many explanations around. One certainly is that state investments, which these debts are used for, do not always earn the yields necessary to pay back these debts. This is part of the nature of public investments. Usually they are not built to earn money in the first place, because they are meant to be for free public use as in roads and schools. More often they stem from a political motivation of spending money to please voters. Nevertheless they are meant to contribute to the prosperity of society. However there is growing evidence that there are negative effects related to their use. Building more roads for instance leads to the creation of more traffic, causing more pollution by emitting greenhouse gases or noise. This again is related to additional *costs* for the repair of negative environmental effects and higher expenses for health care. These costs are usually covered by raising taxes or higher contributions to social insurance systems. These again are factors that impede investments and the hire of employees. Thus they may be leading to higher unemployment, more public expenditure, less tax revenue and so again higher debts. A vicious circle is born, which reaffirms its negative effects.

Another effect of unemployment is a growing difference in wealth in the societies of developed countries, and between nations of the northern hemisphere compared to those in the south. This gap is already causing problems as a result of uncontrollable immigration. Lately we have seen a lot of refugees from Africa risking their lives on trips in small boats to enter the shores of Italy in order to apply for asylum in the European Union. Due to insufficient concepts for integration there are hints that this leads to a growing hostility against those refugees. This might also lead to difficulties in relations between rich and poor nations in general. In the worst case we can expect acts of war as a result of growing discrepancies between north and south with all of their negative consequences.

The social impact of our projects is not always related to the global or local community. First of all we can see impacts on our project team and the users of products of our project. Negative effects in that context could be stress, burn-out and diseases, which damage our own organization in the first place. But they can also be related to negative effects on our society, if they happen on a larger scale. This is why sustainable project management is also vital for those of you who focus on *IT projects* as we will see in section 4.1.2.2 Checklists for *People*.

1.2.2 Environmental Topics

In our search of solutions for economic problems we hear repeatedly that *growth* is the way to go. Despite a steady growth in national products around the world over the last decades, we are still facing economic, environmental and social problems, and they still seem to become more severe. There is a growing awareness that economic development is hurting our natural and social resources. I just described one vicious circle for public investments with negative effects on social prosperity. This again is not only threatening the wellbeing of future generations. More and more it becomes a matter of increasing *costs* in our day. For more than forty years we have been hearing warnings of the effects we will get, if climate change resulting in global warming continues. Scientists tell us that this climate change is caused by burning fossil fuels releasing carbon dioxide into the atmosphere, which then causes a greenhouse effect, heating up our planet. Recently scientists compared their approaches on research about global warming and found out that their different models came to similar results. One of them is that food prices will rise by 20% by the year 2050 due to losses in harvest caused by the effects of global warming (Schrader, 2013). That means that each family in Germany will have to spend €1000 more – in real terms – than they do today.

Figure 1: Drought in Bavaria, Summer 2013

In the summer of 2013 I spent my vacation in Bavaria, the southern part of Germany, which is one of the most fertile areas in Europe. Usually there is an abundance of rainfall, which actually quite often spoilt my vacation when I was a youngster 30 years ago. This year however we had a major drought. Riding my bicycle along the river Isar I found this dry birch tree looking as if it was fall already. I was so appalled to find it here, close to running water in the middle of the year. Hiking around in the mountains where I was used to find creeks and springs with fresh water I saw that actually everything was dry. A single spark would have been enough to ignite a major forest fire. I was quite shocked, because I had never seen that before in our part of world. I have seen dry rivers and dead trees in the deserts of Southern Africa and the Middle East, but not in Central Europe. For me these were proofs that there definitely are changes in our environment right on my doorstep. And I did not like what I saw, because things seem likely to become worse.

Not to like that is one thing. Another one is to think about what these changes will cost me and us. One aspect is mentioned above with the rise of relative prices for food. Another aspect are higher direct costs for the repair of damages caused by natural disasters in the affected areas. Examples of costs to repair environmental damage can be found in reports on the floods of hurricane Katrina of the year 2005, where we find estimated damages with a sum of 200 billion US dollars (Canella, 2007).

Figure 2: New Orleans in the Floods of 2005

In Dresden, the federal state capital of Saxony, Germany, the flood of spring 2013 has caused damages amounting to €100 million to public buildings, schools, streets and bridges. For a population of 500,000 people this means costs of €200 per capita (Sächsische Zeitung, 2013).

50% of the world's population lives within a range of 50 km distance of the seashore. Sea levels are expected to increase by about 1 meter by the end of this century due to global warming. The cost of flood damage in the world's coastal cities by the year 2050 is expected to reach 52 billion US dollars per year! That makes about 10 US dollars for each person living in those areas. Due to the expectation of rising sea levels and the experience of Hurricane Sandy, which caused overall damages estimated at 19 billion US dollars, the City of New York proposed a 20 billion US dollar plan to strengthen the city against such damages. That makes up costs of about 2,400 US dollars per citizen. In the Netherlands more than a quarter of its land lies below sea level. Fortifications and flood management systems cost 9.3 billion US dollars to maintain. That makes up costs of about €700 as a contribution from every individual living in Holland (Guarino, 2013).

There are also figures about the costs of avoiding the necessity of these repair works. There are findings that the stabilization of the world's climate and prevention of further global warming would cost us 1% of the world's social product, i.e. €100 per capita per year (Deutsche Bahn AG, 2013a). That seems quite cheap for people in the western world. It is unaffordable for those living in third world countries. But who actually caused the damage and has been enjoying the advantages of the economic development over the last 100 years?

Other figures say that it would cost 200 billion US dollars by the year 2030 to restructure the economy in order to keep global warming within plus 2° Celsius (Mrusek, 2007). This equals 40 US dollars per capita of the world's population and is of the same order of magnitude as the one mentioned above.

So what actually happens when people and companies recognize their responsibility and take measures to reduce or abolish negative developments? Examples like the initiative of London's Radio Taxi Group to reduce environmental impact by reducing carbon dioxide emissions show that investments in sustainability are actually paying off. In 2005 the operator of chauffeured vehicles invested £100,000, at that time around €150,000, in order to save 24,000 tons of CO_2. That equals costs of €6.25

per ton of CO_2. On the other hand this initiative created new business for the company, by improvements in image and public relations, to the tune of £1.2 million or about €1.8 million (Canella, 2007).

Aside from direct effects and costs we also find indirect ones. A higher frequency of natural disasters like hurricanes in America or floods in Asia has led to higher insurance rates already. These costs are burdening industries like transportation, tourism and real estate, which is not just hurting the organizations but also the people associated with them. This is especially the case in the poorer countries. People there, who are not causing the changes, are more affected by them than those of us in the industrialized rich countries.

Maybe we should reconsider and not be so keen on growth any more. It might be better to replace this goal and paradigm by terms like *change*, *advancement* and particularly *improvement*. These terms are better related to the *quality* of our situation, and not just the *quantity* of amounts of money and things we produce and use.

1.2.3 Economic Topics

We are used to optimizing our businesses by focusing on decreasing costs and increasing revenues in order to become more competitive. For that process we look at monetary items, i.e. we compare prices, and measure our profits and returns on investments in units of currency. From the previous descriptions of social and environmental topics you might have seen that our activities also have effects on areas outside our own. These effects are not yet reflected in the prices we pay or the profits we receive. We call these *external effects*. In the long run however we will be directly affected by these external effects. This is mainly in the form of higher *costs* for investments, insurance and employment of staff.

The goal is now to learn how to avoid these external effects. We want to create positive effects instead, not just for ourselves but for the world around us and the generations following. These positive effects will come back to us in a positive way as well. We will experience lower costs, higher efficiency and a better perception by customers.

One way of avoiding external effects is to measure them, assign values to them and add them to our internal costs. Thus we will be able to assess trade-offs for different approaches to production and service delivery in a sustainability perspective. Section 4.3 on *Eco-Accounting* shows ways and methods to achieve this.

2.   Where do we project managers come in?

Our world is changing rapidly. The world's population is rising. Migration is happening. New ideas and technologies are coming up every day. This leads to new and changed markets and you may find yourself and your organization with new or lost opportunities from one day to another.

For the *adaptation* of business processes to an ever changing society and a challenging competitive environment, *project management* is the tool to manage this change. As leaders in adaptation processes, project managers should be aware of the impact of their activities on their society, environment and business, in short on people, planet and profit. This is what we call the *Triple Bottom Line* (3BL).

Our main goal for economic activities, which project management is part of, is to fulfill the current needs of our societies and organizations. At the same time our activities must not have negative impacts, which are threatening the continuation of our activities or those of future generations. This principle is called *sustainable development* (United Nations, 1987). Therefore we need to look into our tools and methods of project management and where and how this *sustainability* can be supported and measured.

2.1   The Role of Program Management

For project managers alone it will be difficult to establish processes of sustainable project management in their organization. They definitely need support from senior management when it comes to promote the shift from a conventional view of project work to a progressive method of managing your organization's resources without wasting them.

The way to go is to allocate the principles of sustainability in the benefits management of your program management. In program management the strategic priorities of your organization are fixed. These priorities will find their results and benefits in your organization. There are standards for program management where we do have definite processes for benefit realization and sustainment (Project Management Institute, 2013b). An overview of the benefits management processes from *The Standard for Program Management* of the *Project Management Institute* (PMI°) is displayed in *Figure 3: Program Benefits Management*.

The strategic orientation for sustainability of your organization can be justified by its *advantages* in *costs*, progress in competitive advantage and market share, higher motivation of staff, better conditions of work, improved perception by potential customers and advantages in public relations.

Program management itself is mainly concerned to achieve optimized use of human resources in an organization across all projects with familiar goals and topics. With a perspective of sustainability we can extend this goal to optimize the use of human, social, financial and natural resources of your organization. Some of these resources are actually located outside of your organization's area of control. Nevertheless your organization's success is very much dependent on these resources. This is the reason why you should care about them and do everything you can to preserve or even enhance them wherever possible. This is why sustainability is not just a matter for *altruistic* people. It is a mandatory requirement in today's business life and it will become more important with every day that passes.

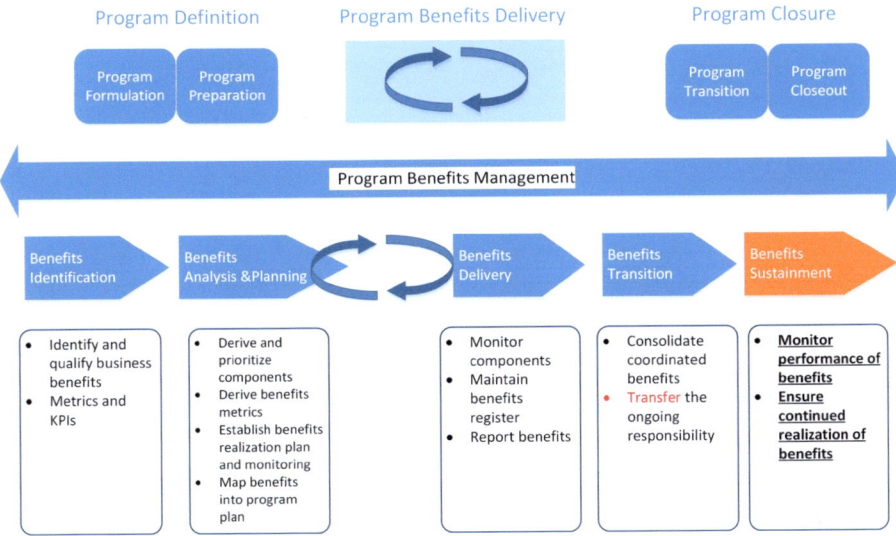

(Project Management Institute, 2013b, p. 35)
Figure 3: Program Benefits Management

Let's have a closer look on the processes of *Benefits Management* in order to gain a better understanding of how this can support you as a project manager. It starts with what we call *Benefits Identification*. In this first step we identify and qualify the benefits that our stakeholders expect to be realized. With respect to sustainability this could be a reduction in energy consumption, lower percentage of sick leave within your workforce, higher tax revenue for your community, constant rate of financial contribution for your product line to your R&D program, etc.

For all these benefits we also need to develop metrics and KPIs in order to keep track of our improvements or fallbacks and for reports to our stakeholders. These will then be documented in what PMI calls a *benefits register*. It helps us to actually communicate our activities, and we as project managers can derive content for our tools in sustainable project management. These tools are described in section 4, *Three Steps to Sustainability*, of this book.

In step two, *Benefits Analysis & Planning*, and three, *Benefits Delivery*, we use the inputs of *Benefits Identification*. We derive specific deliverables and actions for our projects that are supposed to produce the benefits we defined in step one. While producing these benefits we monitor and report our progress. In a process of continuous improvement we review our benefits register for potential changes, improvements or reductions.

An important fourth step is made in *Benefits Transition*. Here our program managers are taking care that our projects' products are transferred to operational areas. Only there can value be delivered by utilizing our benefits in the context of everyday business. It means that this is where improvements desired by our program's stakeholders will have their effects. The results can be an actual reduction in the usage of natural resources, improvements in social resources or higher contributions to profits for certain services and products.

Step five is then to monitor performance of the organization with regard to desired benefits in order to achieve continued sustainability. This process typically gives birth to new projects, which are set up to correct undesired effects or to further improve the level of sustainability reached by previous projects.

This is why sustainability has to start at program level, because these transitions and their sustainment are typically beyond the scope of a single project. Practically spoken our work as project managers usually ends before sustainability can show its effects. Nevertheless it is definitely in our hands to do something essential about sustainability. This will be the topic of the following section 3 "How Can Project Managers Support Sustainable Development?".

2.2   Maturity Classes of Sustainability

When it comes to developing a strategy for sustainability in organizations we typically find five stages of sustainability that range from reactive to proactive (Planko & Silvius, 2012).

In the first stage, *Pre-compliance*, companies or organizations fail to comply with current regulations. This is for example the case when a truck fleet does not conform to prevailing emission regulations. In such a situation companies usually take the next step and change their processes and products in order to comply with prevailing regulations, which is a characteristic of stage two, *Compliance*. A specific action to reach that stage might be to buy trucks with emission class EURO 5 for instance. Another typical action is to stick with current methods or technologies and try to save on their usage. Continuing the truck example, this organization would send their drivers to courses on fuel saving driving practices.

Moving out of this stage two can be done by taking proactive actions for sustainability in different areas of the organization. This is stage three, *Beyond Compliance*. On a small scale, you as a project manager could avoid and reduce traffic by using tools for routing optimization or by consolidating truck loads with other freight forwarders. In project collaboration you could hold teleconferences instead of on site meetings and use sophisticated project collaboration platforms such as *Blue Ant ASP* or *projectplace*. This third stage can often be reached by courageous initiatives of single project managers within their area of control.

The next stage, number four, called *Integrated Strategy*, is then to decide on an overall strategy for the whole organization and coordinate all activities on a corporate level. At this stage program managers should come in as described in the previous section 2.1 "The Role of Program Management". This stage means to rethink your processes and products as a whole for the entire organization with respect to dependencies between different departments. As an example, your company could replace truck transportation with rail or waterway transport. Or you could try to relocate your business closer to suppliers or clients in order to avoid traffic.

Once you reached this stage, there is still one further step to take to reach stage five, which is called *Purpose & Passion*. At this stage companies and organizations are innovative in developing sustainable products and services, not just in order to further increase their profits. They are also driven by responsibility for improvements in society and environment. They want to contribute to a better world. In that case your company would develop new products that hardly need any transportation of the classic kind. This could be achieved by establishing integrated production facilities so close to your customers that they can walk in or visit your shops by riding a bicycle. Another example is to develop a range of products and services which are completely recyclable, without leaving any waste at all, and with a production and distribution process on a zero-emission level.

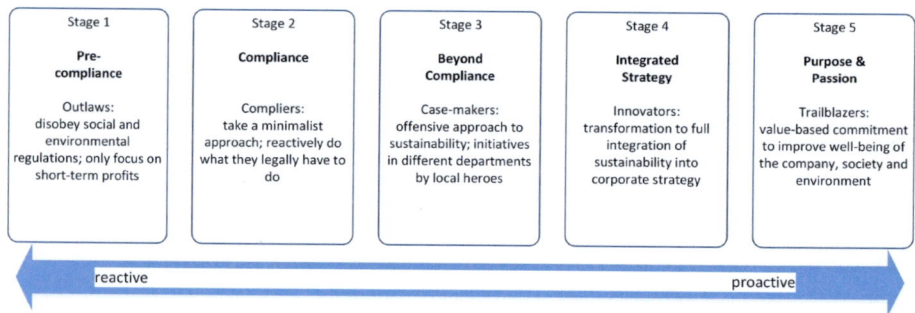

(Planko & Silvius, 2012, p. 13)
Figure 4: Stages of Sustainability

3.   How Can Project Managers Support Sustainable Development?

In section 2.1 and 2.2 we saw how sustainability can be integrated into the overall corporate strategy. Since this book aims to provide a practical guideline for project managers we now come back to the things that they can do for sustainability in managing projects.

What are we actually looking at when we talk about *sustainability*? In order to promote and support *sustainability* in our projects we should focus on enhancing *ecological productivity*. This means that while we are maximizing the added value of our products we strive to minimize the environmental impact. This level of impact can be measured on different levels, with different types of impact and in various phases of the project.

3.1   Levels of Impact

The different *levels of impact* for our assessments are shown in Figure 5. There is a range from personal impacts, to those for the organization, for the indus-try, for the nation and for the international community. It is a pyramid with a broad base at the global level and a narrow top at the personal level.

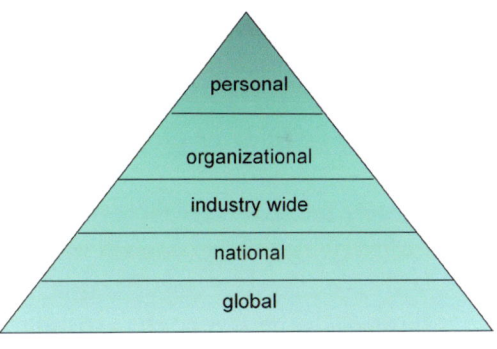

Figure 5: Levels of Impact

This is related to the number of people and other systems that are affected on each level. What I suggest is that we as project managers should work on a top-down approach for sustainability. While it is most important for mankind to have positive impacts on the global level, it is easier to start with those on our personal one.

Personal impacts are those that are easiest to assess and measure because you are exposed to them directly. These impacts most often will give you the motivation to act as a sustainable project manager since you are the one who is actually affected. However they may be least important to your stakeholders, because those things that are important to them might not be affected.

This usually changes when it comes to *organizational impacts*. These are the ones that your program managers and senior management will be most interested in. This is their definite area of control and responsibility. Positive effects on their organization are usually linked to their salary, which turns organizational effects into their own personal impacts. And just like you, senior management is also mostly motivated on this personal level of impact. Therefore responsible persons in the organization or company will also try to create an infrastructure to measure positive effects and impacts on the organizational level. For you, as a project manager committed to promoting sustainability, this means that it will help if you focus on these organizational impacts when filing a business case for your sustainable project.

Closely related to impacts on the organizational level are those on the industry. Anything you do for sustainability in your area of business will have effects on organizations and companies that are doing a similar business. When we act in a sustainable way we always bear in mind that it will not just help the environment. We are convinced that it actually will also sharpen our competitive edge, because we will save *costs* in the long run and it will improve our perception by customers and other interested parties. So when we are making progress in sustainability our competitors will have to react. Otherwise they are going to constantly lose business to us. Another industry-wide effect will be caused by staff switching from one company to another. This usually happens between companies of the same industry. Once we act sustainably we will see that the motivation of our staff will rise and staff fluctuation will decrease. However, sometimes people leave a company for other personal reasons than dissatisfaction with their employer. They might look for a promotion you cannot offer or they have to relocate due to personal reasons. In that case they will take their experiences in sustainability with them. Thus sustainability will spread further over your industry.

When more and more companies of one industry sector act sustainably it will spark sustainable changes in other sectors as well, because staff and customers increasingly become aware of sustainable topics and start to ask for sustainable products and services for all aspects of their lives. This is the way how changes on a *national level* will be induced.

The same forces driving that change on a national level will lead to changes on a *global level*. Our activities will change markets not just because we are developing different offerings for current and potential customers. Our demand in goods and services as inputs to our production processes will change as well. And this is why competitors and suppliers will have incentives to adapt and become players in sustainability as well. Since our companies in the industrialized world of Central Europe and North America most often find their suppliers in other hemispheres around the world, we can lead the transformation to a global sustainable economy.

Once we go beyond the organizational level it will be more difficult to measure impacts on sustainability. How can you measure whether your industry is producing less waste, uses less water and fossil fuels? In some cases like emissions of carbon dioxide there are reports on a national or industry level published by governmental organizations. Nevertheless progress in sustainability beyond our own organization is something we definitely want to achieve. And we can actually use it for the wellbeing of our own organization by working on our public relations and actively communicating positive effects of our activities on entities in our environment, e.g. less noise, lower emissions, higher contributions to our community etc.

The top-down approach described above is a proactive way of working on sustainability in your projects. You recognize the need to change something. Then you start in your personal environment and work on inducing positive changes in outer circles. In the first stage this awareness that changes are necessary is usually caused by deteriorations of entities which you are not directly affected by. You learn about environmental problems in Bangladesh, social problems in Africa, effects of the ozone hole in Australia, increasing prices for food due to shortages in natural resources. You learn about the root cause and about interactions and you become aware of your role in the system. And then you start to work from the top down.

In many situations your organization will be forced to change to sustainable processes. This is when others e.g. on a global level have come to the conclusion that we urgently need a reduction in carbon dioxide emissions in order to stop the irreparable effects of global warming. The UK Government in 2013 passed a law that requires all British companies listed on the London Stock Exchange or the New York stock markets to publish their carbon dioxide emissions (Department for Environment, Food and Rural Affairs, 2013a). The topic is called *mandatory carbon reporting*. Even if you are not working for such a British company you may be obliged to report your own emissions because you work as a supplier for them.

Current environmental changes might also lead the United Nations or G-20 countries to decide on a resolution binding on their members to actually achieve a certain goal in emissions reduction. This will trickle down through different levels of legislative bodies like the European

Parliament and finally reach your organization in the form of a law that you have to obey or a tax you have to pay. This is a *bottom-up process*, from global awareness to forced personal reaction. As you will agree, a company that waits until it is forced to act might have saved some money while it waited. However the company that acted proactively will have reached a competitive advantage and maybe even a unique selling point by that point in time. And this will outweigh potential short term cost savings in most cases.

3.2   Types of Impact

As mentioned before the Triple Bottom Line includes three different *types of impacts*:

- Those on *people*, i.e. on social relationships and individual health.
- Outputs related to our *planet*, i.e. environmental topics that come to mind first, when we think about sustainability.
- Impacts on *profits*, i.e. on numbers, measured in units of currencies, which we can calculate for our organization or business.

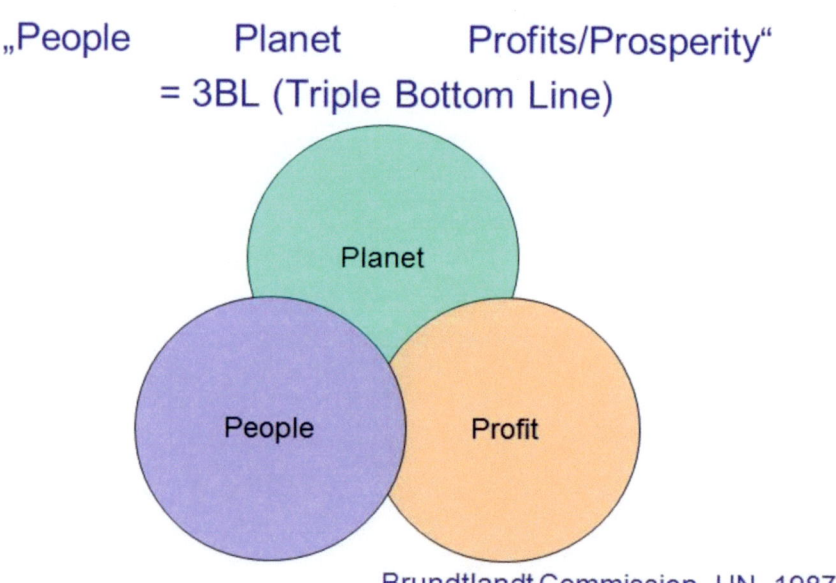

Figure 6: Triple Bottom Line

The first category, *people*, includes the staff we are working with or people who are affected by the project. These are customers or users of our deliverables. They all belong to our local, national or international society. Common topics for impacts on *people* are labor practices, community support or human rights that we can preserve, improve or impair through our projects. Techniques for gathering and assessing impacts on *people* are known from exercises in stakeholder management, which forms part of project management processes and has become a knowledge area of its own in the new PMBoK® 5th Edition (Project Management Institute, 2013a).

The next category, *planet*, includes all impacts on what we usually understand as the natural environment. Topics here are ecology, energy, waste, transportation, water, etc.

Profit is the heading for all topics affecting the economic value of our enterprise or organization. These are the numbers that we are used to working with, like ROI, turnover, profit, cost rates, etc. Effects on *profit* are quite obvious in most cases. And they are easy to measure, because we receive specific numbers for their values. So we can see what gets better or worse immediately. We can compare, sum up and so on.

Impacts on *people* and *planet* are more complicated to measure. It is difficult to make assessments for social factors on a metric scale. We could use GDP per capita, number of inhabitants per physician or divorce rates as indicators of social wellbeing. These indicators are published in absolute numbers that we can work with and measure impacts on *people*.

For impacts on *planet*, i.e. our natural environment, the concentration of atmospheric carbon dioxide has become quite a popular indicator. You can get estimates of CO_2 emissions for almost any means of transportation or source of energy. Other indicators to watch can be the concentration of toxic substances in water or waste emitted by our production processes.

Avoiding or minimizing negative impacts on *people* and *planet* will have direct positive effects on your cost rates, your perception in the market, and motivation of your staff. These are directly related to positive effects on *profit*.

However, the direct effect of your project activities on *people*, *planet*, and *profit* is not always easy to track and measure. Indicators may not be available on time. To begin with it might be too costly to find specialists for these assessments. Know-how on your side might not be sufficient in order to come up with reliable numbers. Therefore we use a three-stage-model called *Three Steps to Sustainability*. It takes us from a rough estimate to an elaborate qualitative assessment, and finally to quantitative methods of calculating the level of sustainability in your projects.

3.3   Systemic Approach

As you can see from the descriptions of levels and types of impact, project managers who are working sustainably need to have a broader view of the effects and implications of their projects. In order to be successful the whole discipline of project management needs to be more contextually oriented. Since the 1950s project management has been based on a paradigm that projects are a closed system and anything that happens in a project is controllable by the project manager. Since then we have been trained to focus on scope, time and costs. The *magic triangle* is the concept for managing changes in our projects.

Starting in the 1990s there has been a change in that paradigm. The view on project management has been shifting to a focus on organizational changes implied and connected to projects. When you assess the role of a project in an organizational change you naturally come across topics of sustainability. Instead of scope, time, cost we focus on people, planet, profit. Project management processes are not just initiation – planning

– execution – closing. We also have to consider the full product lifecycle of design – develop – manufacture – operate – decommission – disposal (Silvius & Schipper, Sustainability and Projects, 2012).

Figure 7: Sustainability in Projects shows a conceptual comparison between conventional project management and sustainable development. In a combination of both, i.e. project management for sustainable projects, both lifecycle orientation and assessments for impacts on people, planet and profit require a more systemic approach to project management, especially when it comes to assessments with regard to different levels of impact. Systemic in this context means that project managers are looking at impacts between entities, their interactions and – very important – *repercussions* between them.

Sustainability in Projects

Sustainable Development	vs.	Conventional Project Management
Long-term oriented		Short-term oriented
Interest of future generations		Interest of sponsors and stakeholders
Life-cycle oriented		Deliverable oriented
People, planet, profit		Scope, time, cost
Increasing complexity		Reduced complexity

Silvius, G.; Schipper, R: Sustainability and Projects, 2012

Figure 7: Sustainability in Projects

Figure 8: *Network of Impacts* gives an example of such a systemic assessment. In the model used here we distinguish between three modeling levels: *entity*, *activity* and *indicator*. The first, *entity*, represents the different elements of the *Triple Bottom Line*. In our model we have *society* as part of *people*, *nature* representing *planet* and an *enterprise* for *profit*.

On the next level down, every entity executes certain activities. In our example we look at a *society* that has an increased use of renewable energies. *Nature* is exposed to global warming and creates natural disasters and the *enterprise* in this model is active in gathering and exploiting natural gas.

Activities of entities do have effects on *indicators*. These effects are measurable. Indicators are specific for each entity and have positive or negative effects on them. In this way indicators are used to measure the state or wellbeing of the entity. In our case society is measured with *wealth in household income*, which has a positive relationship with the wellbeing of society. Nature has the indicator *atmospheric CO_2* with a negative effect on it and our sample enterprise is measured in terms of *turnover* and *cost*. The former is positively and the latter negatively correlated to the enterprise.

The basis for the combination of these correlations is simple mathematics. We know that plus times plus is plus and plus times minus is minus. In our case we start with a favorable effect for an enterprise that is drilling for natural gas. This enterprise is experiencing an increase in gas gathering, which has a positive effect on turnover. This is marked with the green arrow. Turnover itself is positively related to the wellbeing of the entity enterprise. This is marked with a "+". Therefore the effect of this increase is positive as a whole.

In our model the entities *society* and *enterprise* are related like in the classic economic models. People from *society* work for the *enterprise* and are thus participating in the *enterprise's* wellbeing or decline. Therefore the increase in turnover is also positively related to wealth measured in household income (green arrow), and household income is positively related to wealth in society (+). Therefore we still have a positive effect, because the combination of + and + and + and + is positive.

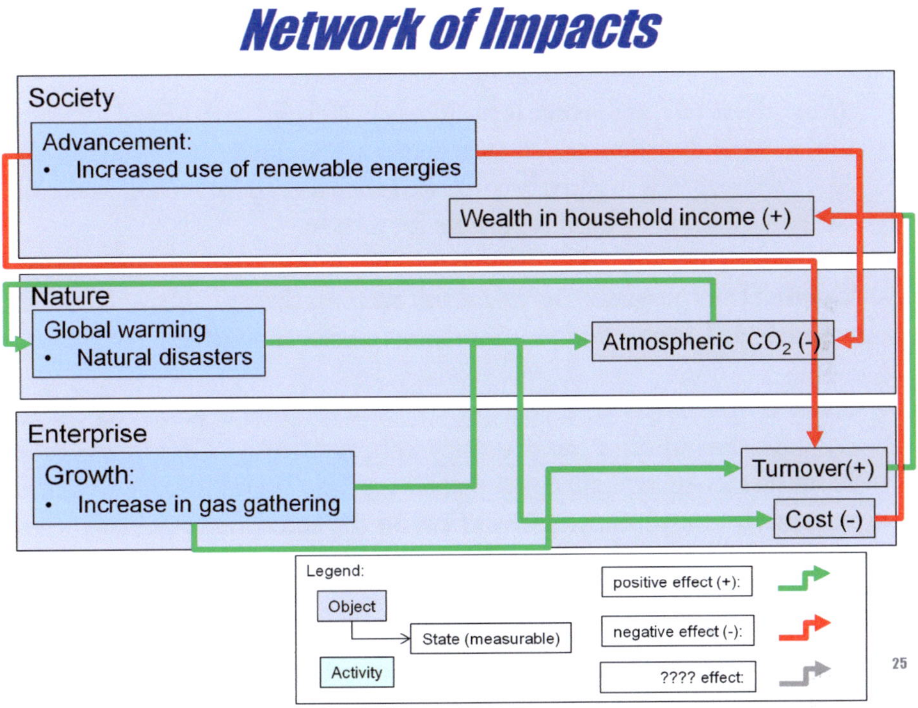

Network of Impacts

Figure 8: Network of Impacts

The same increase of gas gathering and use of gas itself leads to an increase in atmospheric carbon dioxide. The correlation is positive. Therefore we have the green arrow between this activity *gas gathering* and the indicator *atmospheric CO_2*. However the effect of more carbon dioxide in the atmosphere is negative. Therefore the combination of both has a negative effect.

When we look at the entity *society* we find the activity *increased use of renewable energies*. This activity is negatively correlated with the indicator *atmospheric CO_2*, which itself has a negative effect. Minus times minus is plus and therefore we do have a positive effect here. However our activity *increased use of renewable energies* does have a negative effect on the turnover of the enterprise whose business is the gathering of gas. Turnover has a "+" and so the effect of the activity on the entity is negative.

Atmospheric CO_2 as a whole is positively correlated with global warming and natural disasters, which themselves are negative. *Increased use of renewable energies* is negatively correlated with *atmospheric CO_2*. Therefore the combination of both is positive for *nature*.

Coming from *gas gathering* to *natural disasters* through *atmospheric CO_2* we have plus, minus and plus resulting in a negative effect.

Natural disasters as an activity of the entity *nature* is positively correlated with the indicator *cost* of *enterprise* (green arrow). Cost on the other hand has a negative effect on the enterprise. Therefore an increase of natural disasters has a negative effect on the enterprise. And this is also negatively correlated with wealth in society shown by the red arrow to household income.

The overall effect of an increase of gas gathering on society in this model is therefore negative. The effect of increased use of renewable energies on society is ambivalent: it is negative due to the negative effect on *turnover*. And it is positive due to the reduction of costs. It is now a matter of comparing the actual value of these two effects in order to come to a conclusion of what is best for society. This can be done with the help of methods for eco-accounting as described in section 4.3.

This simple modeling technique can help you to make assessments of effects inside and outside of your projects. It is sometimes quite surprising to see what kind of overall effect you get when you combine all correlations between the start and the final point of your analysis.

3.4   Process Groups and Knowledge Areas

Project Managers who are working according to the PMI˙ standard called Project Management Body of Knowledge, in short PMBoK˙ (Project Management Institute, 2013a) distinguish between five *process groups*, which are applied throughout the *project life cycle*.

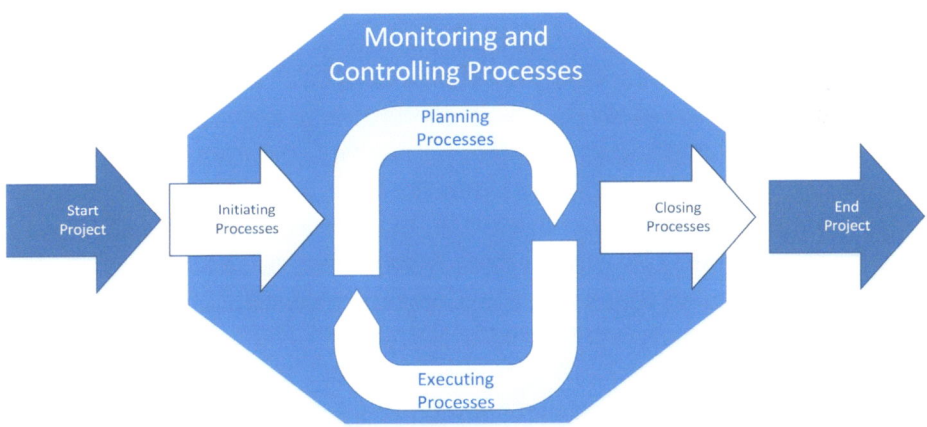

Figure 9: Project Management Process Groups

Figure 9: *Project Management Process Groups* shows the relationships between those processes and their role in the project life cycle.

In the following sections you will find a description of those processes, in which specific tools or methods for sustainability can be applied.

Table 2: *Process Groups for Sustainability* on page 54 shows an overview of the project management process groups. The processes suitable for sustainable methods are highlighted in green.

3.4.1 Project Initiation

A first step to sustainability can be taken when you lay the foundation of the project during project initiation. In the PMBoK˚ these processes are described in the knowledge area *Develop Project Charter*. In this step the project receives its direction, purpose and the goals, which need to be achieved. When an organization has a high level of maturity, it has a strategy and specific documented goals for sustainability which can be taken as a reference. They should now be applied to the project charter and become part of the project's business case. In a best case scenario your program management or project sponsor will incorporate these topics in the project charter. If this is not the case you as the project manager can take the initiative and work on incorporating sustainability goals. You can use the *Checklist Criteria* from section 4.1.2 in order to derive substantial goals of sustainability for your project and give it a direction towards improvements in sustainability.

Once you finished the charter of your project it is time to decide on the best approach for achieving the goals that have been set for it. The *Scoring System* in section 4.2 can help you to prioritize between different project alternatives. It is a qualitative method enabling you to compare potential actions on the basis of combined and weighted attributes.

When you want to further optimize the results of your project for sustainability, our methods of *Eco-Accounting* described in section 4.3 can be used to support your business case for sustainability with monetary values.

According to PMI® the project charter is input to the next important step in project initiation, which is to *Identify Stakeholders* (Project Management Institute, 2013a, p. 394). The role of stakeholders typically is more important in sustainable projects than it is in conventional ones. Stakeholders are people, and *people* is one of the categories of the *Triple Bottom Line*. The purpose of our activities aiming at sustainability is to avoid negative effects and enhance positive outcomes for the people related to our project. The *Checklist Criteria* in section 4.1.2 will help you to identify all relevant stakeholders for your sustainable project.

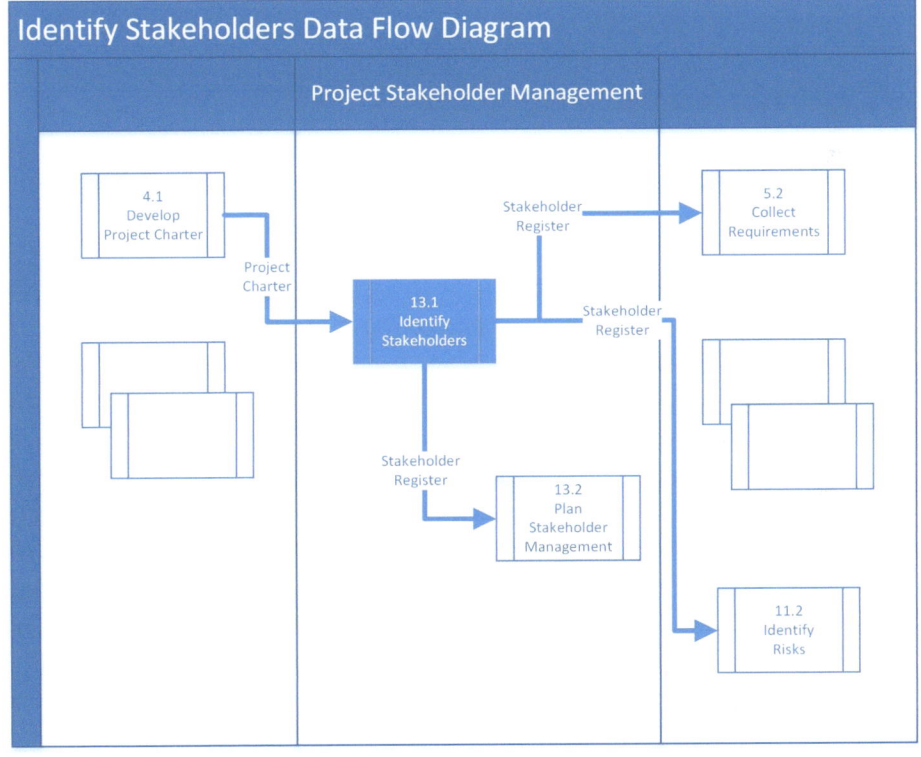

Figure 10: Identify Stakeholders Data Flow Diagram

With the process of *Identify Stakeholders* project initiation can be concluded. Outputs of this phase like the *project charter* and the *stakeholder register* are inputs to project planning. This is visualized in data flow diagrams that we find in the PMBoK˙. The one for *Identify Stakeholders* is displayed in part in Figure 10: *Identify Stakeholders Data Flow Diagram*. It describes the relationship between project charter, stakeholders, requirements and risks. The dependencies between these entities support the importance of the project charter, where the goals for sustainability are documented.

A comprehensive set of goals leads to an expansive stakeholder register and a good coverage of *people*, which leads to a sufficient set of requirements and a useful risk register. All of these outputs and inputs of project management contribute to the overall success of conventional and sustainable projects.

3.4.2 Project Planning

3.4.2.1 Scope Management

An essential step in project planning for sustainability is to *Collect Requirements*. It builds on the project charter and stakeholder register from project initiation and produces *requirement documentation*. This is the perfect point for the introduction of requirements for sustainability, because now we can actually define what the products and outcomes of our project shall be like. Of course this should be a sustainable product or an outcome contributing to sustainability. At least the execution of our project should have no negative effects on sustainability. As in project initiation, you can use the *Checklist Criteria* from section 4.1.2 in order to find relevant requirements for your project.

The next step in project planning is then to actually define the project's outputs and products in the process *Define Scope*. Since all the requirements for sustainability have been documented before in *Collect Requirements* there is no need for the application of specific, sustainable methods in this step. It is only important to consistently implement the sustainable requirements. This might become difficult in an environment that is not used to these topics. Sometimes sustainability is more costly than conventional methods. Good arguments are needed to convince project sponsors and team members to actually support sustainability. Methods of eco-accounting from section 4.3 can help you to come up with concrete numbers. Balancing reasons for one or the other part of sustainable scope is supported by methods of our Scoring System in section 4.2.

Once the scope is defined it needs to be broken down into deliverables and manageable activities. This is what the process of *Create WBS* is all about. As with *Define Scope*, we don't necessarily need specific methods of sustainability here. All the requirements have been set before and need to be implemented here.

3.4.2.2 Time Management

Based on the scope that has been developed in *Project Scope Management* we can now continue our planning processes with *Project Time Management*. In this knowledge area we *Define Activities* according to the deliverables of our work breakdown structure (WBS) from *Create WBS*. These activities are then brought into useful sequence. After that resources and durations for activities are estimated. Finally, based on this information, a schedule is developed.

Since our activities in this schedule are aiming at fulfilling the requirements for sustainability, which we defined in *Project Scope Management*, we don't have to add anything specific for sustainability in the processes of *Project Time Management*.

3.4.2.3 Risk Management

Before we come to *Project Cost Management* we should have a look at the implications of sustainability on *Risk Management*. This is another area of project management where we can apply the principles of sustainability (Gale, The Real Deal, 2009b). First of all when you *Plan Risk Management*, you should make a decision to incorporate the topics of sustainability in the risk management process of your projects. Our *Checklist Criteria* in section 4.1.2 can help you to *Identify Risks* and to produce a comprehensive list of risks related to sustainability, the so-called *risk register*. This list may include risks on categories like the ones we already discussed, such as higher costs for environmental damage, human sickness and societal disruption, which might all be related to a downturn in financial success. Thus your organization's profits may be directly related to these risks.

In the next step of *Project Risk Management*, when you *Perform Qualitative Risk Analysis* the *Scoring System* of section 4.2 supports the procedure of weighting and prioritizing the risks of sustainability. When you finally assess the potential costs of the most important risks of your project and *Perform Quantitative Risk Analysis* you can use the methods of *Eco-Accounting* described in section 4.3.

3.4.2.4 Cost Management

The outputs of *Project Scope Management*, *Project Time Management*, and *Project Risk Management* can be used in *Project Cost Management* (Project Management Institute, 2013a, p. 201). In the process of *Estimate Costs* project managers calculate the financial resources they need to complete project activities. This is based upon the *Work Breakdown Structure* we created during *Project Scope Management* and the risk register we produced during *Identify Risks*, as we can see in Figure 11: *Estimate Costs Data Flow Diagram*.

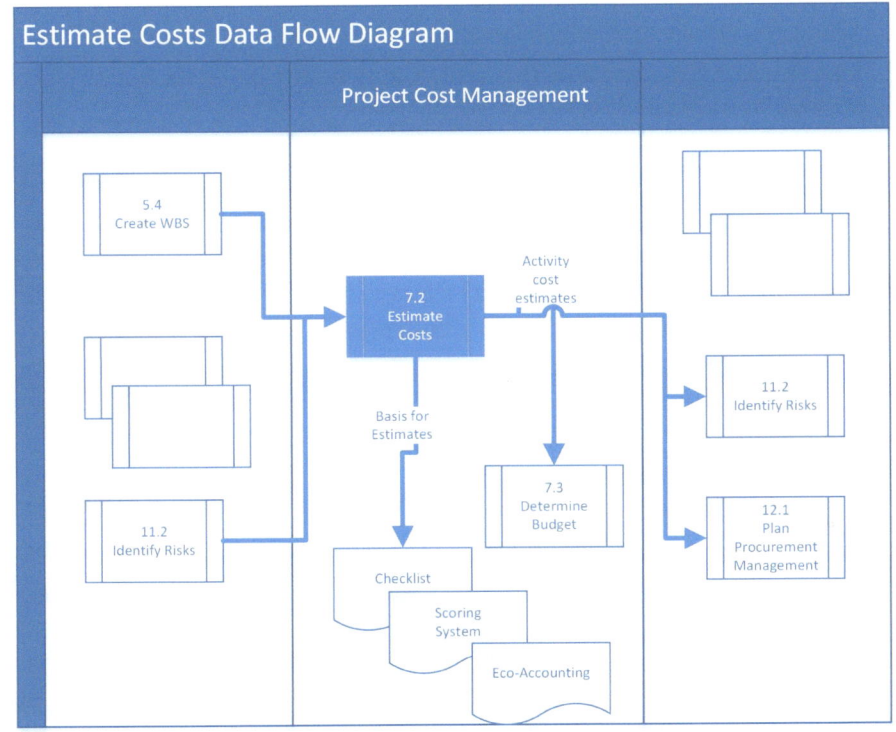

Figure 11: Estimate Costs Data Flow Diagram

For *Estimate Costs* you can use qualitative criteria like the ones that are described in 4.1 *Checklists* and 4.2 *Scoring System* in order to assess the real costs caused by our project. In that case you will take the conventional monetary values of your cost estimates and add the costs of conformance and nonconformance. This technique is called *Cost of Quality (CoQ)* (Project Management Institute, 2013a, p. 206). It is also described in section 3.4.2.6 *Greenality: Sustainability and Quality* on page 45. You might conduct a three point estimate for instance and add the CoQs to the pessimistic values. In a holistic assessment you should also calculate the mid term and long term savings of your sustainable actions. Otherwise you might lose the business case.

Once you have achieved a higher level of maturity in sustainability you can also directly apply actual monetary values like the ones we developed in section 4.3 *Eco-Accounting*.

Outputs of *Estimate Costs*, i.e. *activity cost estimates*, can be used to go back to *Identify Risks* and review the risk register. In the so-called *basis for estimates*, which are also an output of *Estimate Costs*, you can file additional documentation about the conditions for cost estimates like assumptions and constraints. This information can be used to revise your checklist, scoring system and eco-accounting already in use.

3.4.2.5 Procurement Management

Activity cost estimates from *Cost Management* will also be used for the process of *Plan Procurement Management*. In addition this process uses the input of *Scope, Risk* and *Stakeholder Management* as can be seen in Figure 12: *Plan Procurement Management Data Flow Diagram*. It is dependent on the processes of *Collect Requirements, Identify Risks* and *Identify Stakeholders* and also provides feedback to *Risk* and *Stakeholder Management* (Project Management Institute, 2013a, p. 359). All of these processes and knowledge groups are relevant to the application of sustainable tools and methods as described here.

In *Project Procurement Management* the focus for sustainability is on the process group *Plan Procurement Management*. Here we have the opportunity to lay the foundation for decisions in favor of sustainability that will be made in the process of *Conduct Procurements*. Potential changes and corrections towards sustainability can be made during *Control Procurements*.

In *Plan Procurement Management* aspects of sustainability can be applied during *Make-or-Buy-Analysis*. In this technique the intrinsic capabilities and capacities of an organization to contribute sustainable products and services for the project are rated. All related costs, i.e. direct and indirect costs, are to be considered (Project Management Institute, 2013a, p. 365). This is the point where especially indirect costs related to sustainability should be included in our considerations. Methods of eco-accounting can help with these. Altogether we might find that there is neither sufficient capability nor capacity within our organization to deliver a product or service in a sustainable way. This is when a buy-decision is made. The *Market Research* technique will help you to find adequate sustainable suppliers outside your organization.

These buy-decisions and information on potential suppliers will then be found in outputs like *Procurement Statement of Work, Procurement Documents* and *Source Selection Criteria*. All these documents will reflect requirements for potential sellers to deliver sustainable services and products. These requirements can be derived by using the *Checklists* from section 4.1. Decisions and trade-offs between different alternative providers, services and products can also be reached by using methods of the *Scoring System* from section 4.2 and *Eco-Accounting* from section 4.3.

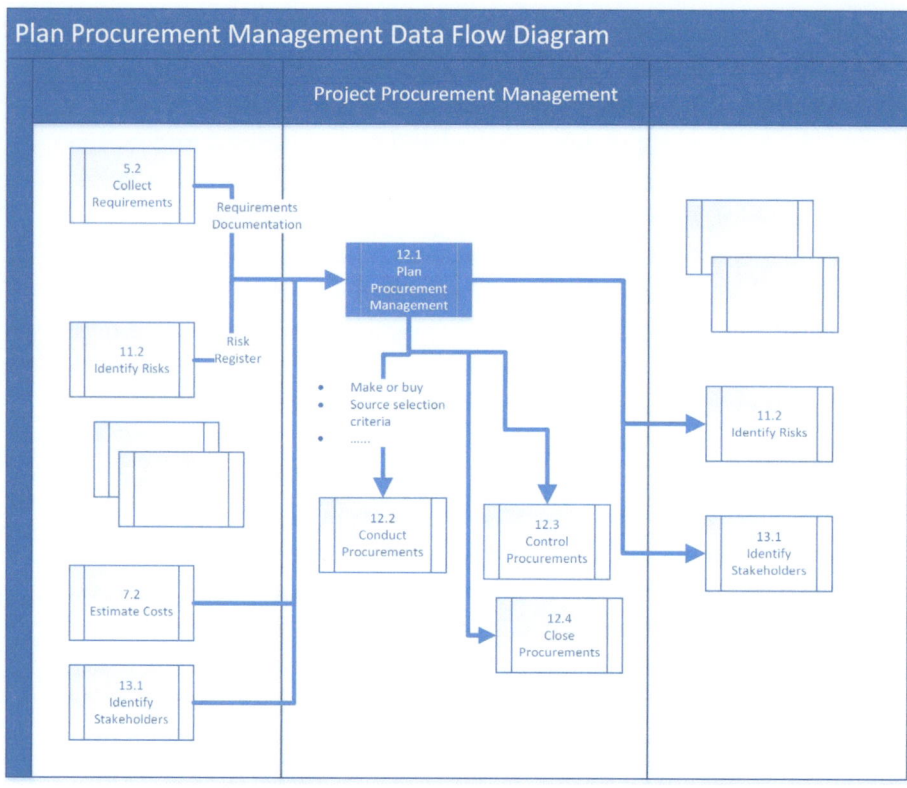

Figure 12: Plan Procurement Management Data Flow Diagram

Another helpful tool for rating and selecting sellers in Procurement Management is the *Four Levels of Sustainable Committed Sellers*. *Sustainable Committed Sellers* (SCSs) are providers of goods or services, who have committed themselves to operating their businesses on the basis of sustainable principles (Deland, 2009). The different levels are described and distinguished as follows.

Level 1: Consists of sellers and suppliers providing sustainable resource alternatives.

Level 2: Consists of sellers and suppliers who are willing to integrate sustainability into their businesses. They work with the buyer to learn and grow in order to operate sustainably.

Level 3: Consists of sellers and suppliers who meet the requirements of Level 1 and 2. Beyond that they have a plan for *Corporate Sustainability* which already shows some measurable results in reducing the environmental footprint. Level 3 SCSs act with a willingness to report and further improve these results.

There is a standard to support this reporting. The Global Reporting Initiative (GRI) issues so-called *Sustainability Reporting Guidelines* (Global Reporting Initiative (TM), 2013) which can be used to structure these reports. For buyers of goods and services this structure is helpful for finding the information needed about the SCS.

Finally Level 4 consists of sellers and suppliers exhibiting characteristics of Level 1 through 3 plus a persuasive commitment towards sustainability in the organization. This commitment is documented in plans and processes of continuous improvement, regular reporting, staff involvement, etc.

3.4.2.6 Greenality: Sustainability and Quality

Education and training of modern project managers is usually based on international standards as found in Prince2, ISO 21500 promoted by the International Project Management Association (IPMA) (Wagner, 2012) or the Project Management Body of Knowledge (PMBoK®) by the Project Management Institute (PMI®). However, these available standards do not address the topics of sustainability adequately (Eid, 2009). Still project management and sustainability are seen as being of a different nature, as you have seen in Figure 7: *Sustainability in Projects* on page 31.

In their book *Green Project Management* the authors Richard Maltzman and David Shirley suggest that we should integrate aspects of sustainability into the quality management of our projects (Maltzman & Shirley, 2011). They call this *greenality* as the combination of green aspects and quality management.

Integrating sustainability into quality management makes perfect sense. In PMI®'s PMBoK® Guide (5th edition) *Project Quality Management* is defined as the processes necessary in order to satisfy the needs for which it was undertaken. It also supports continuous improvement of the organization (Project Management Institute, 2013a, p. 227). The overall strategy for the way to sustainability should be fixed in the program management of your organization as described in section *2.1* on program management. The goals for your project can be derived from this strategy. These goals should then be reflected in our activities of quality management. It provides us with the *Seven Basic Quality Tools* for measuring our deliverables with regard to the specifications we have defined. *Cause-and-effect diagrams*, *checksheets*, and *control charts* are especially useful for supporting methods of sustainability. In a nutshell, quality management is about fitness for purpose and harmonizing with requirements. Sustainability will be the basis for many requirements that your project has to meet, as we will see in Section 4 *Three Steps to Sustainability*.

The first step in quality management is to identify the standards and requirements to be used. This happens during the process of *Plan Quality Management*. After this planning process we have *Perform Quality Assurance* and *Control Quality*, i.e. to monitor and record results of quality activities in order to assess performance and initiate necessary changes.

The basic principles of quality management in the PMBoK®, which can also be applied to the purpose of enhancing sustainability, are

- customer satisfaction,
- prevention over inspection,
- management responsibility, and
- cost of quality.

Customer satisfaction is about management of requirements. In our case of sustainability we have to ensure that our products are not just adequate for the needs of our customers. We also need to take care of the impacts our products and services have on people, planet and profits as described in the previous sections.

Prevention over inspection means that quality – and for us sustainability as well – has to be designed and built into our projects' deliverables. This corresponds to the thoughts in section *2.2 Maturity Classes of Sustainability*. Higher maturity is reached, when you start to develop a product from the end of its lifecycle. That means avoiding negative impacts from the very beginning instead of dealing with negative impacts once they have occurred. This can be achieved by deliverables that can be re-used or easily recycled rather than causing waste, which has to be disposed of.

Management responsibility means that success in greenality is related to support by senior management. It has to take responsibility and provide you with "suitable resources at adequate capacities" (Project Management Institute, 2013a, p. 229). Any other approach, like bottom-up from project management to senior management, will easily fail, because sustainability requires at least a minimum of anticipation. If you want to act as a sustainable project manager when lacking that management support, you should be aware of this obstacle and not waste too much energy on your efforts. Nevertheless the politics of persistent and small steps towards this goal will bring the desired success in the end.

Cost of Conformance	Cost of Nonconformance
Prevention Costs (Build a quality product) • Training • Document processes • Equipment • Time to do it right • *Checklists* **Appraisal Costs** (Assess the quality) • Testing • *Eco-accounting* • *CO_2- reporting*	**Internal Failure Costs** (Failures found by the project) • Rework • Scrap • *Sickness leave due to unhealthy working conditions* **External Failure Costs** (Failures found by the customer) • *Liabilities* • Warranty work • Lost business • *Waste* • *Negative perception*
Money spent during the project **to avoid failures**	Money spent during and after the project **because of failures**

(Project Management Institute, 2013a, p. 235)

Table 1: Cost of Quality

The concept *Cost of Quality (COQ)* is quite useful to promote the topics of sustainability. It refers to costs of conformance and costs of nonconformance to requirements. *Costs of conformance* are related to the fact that the execution of projects with a focus on sustainability usually implies higher investments than for conventional projects. Sustainable project managers need to make more elaborate assessments. Their business cases need additional work for aspects of sustainability. You need special human and technical resources for that. It will take more time and so on. On the other hand COQ also includes *costs of nonconformance*. In conventional projects these costs are made up of *internal failure costs* like reworking and scrapping and *external failure costs* for warranty work, liabilities and lost business (Project Management Institute, 2013a, p. 235). With a sustainability perspective we could have induced sick leave and higher costs of waste disposal as internal costs, and liabilities for repair of ecological damages and negative perception by customers due to non-compliance to ecological principles as external costs. Some of these costs we already discussed in section *1.2 Current Problems*.

Table 1: Cost *of Quality* shows examples for specific costs of conformance and nonconformance. Originally this table was used in the PMBoK®. Specific costs with relation to sustainability have been added in green italics.

The costs of nonconformance, which are related to non-compliance with sustainability, can be further analyzed in risk management. Each company will make its own *cost-benefit analysis* for sustainable projects. It will be based on their special situation in the market and society. Some of them accept higher stakes than others. In that case let's hope that they will take the risk of investing in sustainable processes and products rather than accepting the risks of non-compliance.

3.4.3   Project Execution

3.4.3.1 Human Resource Management

After planning for the sustainable project is finished, it will move on to the execution part, just like any conventional project. For *Project Execution* we want to begin by examining the relationship of processes in *Human Resource Management* to sustainability.

It starts with *Develop Project Team*. In the PMBoK® this is a process of improving team competencies and the overall team environment to enhance project performance (Project Management Institute, 2013a,

p. 273). As key benefits from this process we find – amongst others – enhanced competencies, motivated employees, and reduced staff turnover rates. These are the same goals and impacts on *people* we want to achieve with our sustainable projects. Human resources, and with it the dimension *people* from the Triple Bottom Line, is the most important factor for *IT-projects*. In IT many projects do not have a measurable effect on the global community or the environment. Here the project team is in the focus of our activities for sustainability. Criteria for sustainability with regard to people can be found in our checklist section 4.1.2.2 on *People*. Most important here are topics like healthy work environment, work-life balance, challenging but achievable goals, supporting personal strengths, etc.

Develop Project Team is based on *Plan Human Resource Management* in Project Planning and *Acquire Project Team* in Project Execution. Specifics of sustainability can be included in the *human resource management plan*. Part of this plan is the *staffing management plan*. It defines the training needs and recognition and reward mechanisms for the project team (Project Management Institute, 2013a, p. 266). For the training needs we can include competencies of sustainability like awareness training and application training for methods and tools of sustainability. For recognition and reward we should include sustainability measures like reduced travel and expenses related to CO_2 emissions.

In *Acquire Project Team* the staffing management plan has to be executed. It is important to build a competent and effective team. In order to find the right people for the sustainability job it is important to have existing information on the related competencies of people (Project Management Institute, 2013a, p. 269). Therefore it is good to adapt the *enterprise environmental factors* of your organization according to this requirement. It is advisable to update your *human resource database* by adding attributes for competencies like sustainable project management, experience in sustainable projects, knowledge of sustainable technologies, predilection for energy saving, willingness to travel by train instead of plane, etc.

Virtual teams are part of the tools and techniques for *Acquire Project Team* (Project Management Institute, 2013a, p. 271). The virtualization of IT resources may save up to 80% of CO_2 emissions (Binary Artworks, 2013, p. 6). Similarly to that, the virtualization of teams may do the same. Think about using collaboration platforms like *projectplace extended* or *Blue Ant ASP* in order to create a team from different geographic regions. It can save traveling costs and related emissions. It will not just help you to save money and contribute to a sustainable working environment. In many cases it will be the only way of integrating certain specialists with specific knowledge into your project team.

In *Develop Project Team* you finally perform the activities which have been planned before. This process uses tools and techniques like training, team-building, colocation, and recognition and rewards (Project Management Institute, 2013a, p. 275-277). All of these may and should include aspects of sustainability as explained before: training should be conducted with a focus on awareness of the impacts of projects on the Triple Bottom Line. In team-building we can build upon this awareness and aim at a common perception of the team as to why it is important to work sustainably. The group interaction will induce a special drive and release the right energy within the team. This team-building is quite important in case you decide to work with a virtual team. Such a team should have met at least once in the early phase of the project in order to form a really powerful team. Finally the motivated and successful team should be rewarded and recognized for its accomplishments in sustainability. Here again our methods of scoring and eco-accounting can help to measure this.

3.4.3.2 Stakeholder Management and Communication

Stakeholder management and communication of your project's progress is just as important in the area of sustainability as in conventional projects. Good communication with *stakeholders outside the project team* will help you to gain the necessary support, which is needed for the changes your project will trigger. Switching to sustainability may seem difficult for many of the persons affected because they have to leave their comfort zone and change their usual habits. Therefore we have to be frank with our stakeholders about what we are doing in the project, the effects it will have and of course the benefits and the value it will create.

It is also important to keep your *sponsors* updated. In many cases sustainable projects will cause higher initial *costs* and efforts than conventional projects. Therefore you need to make a good case for your sponsor as to why it is actually worth making this investment. Of course we will document that in a business case during project initiation. In a very mature sustainable organization project managers will also receive their project charter with goals for sustainability from their program management. Even then we constantly need to communicate our goals and progress in order to stabilize our sponsors' conviction. We need to provide them with viable information, which they can use when they are asked about sustainable actions in their organization.

Last but not least, project managers need to take care to inform their staff about activities contributing to sustainability. This will not just enhance their motivation. It also helps to avoid potential flaws in the future and may generate initiatives for further improvements (HAVI Logistics GmbH, 2010, p. 12).
In Project Execution these activities are related to the processes of *Manage Communications* and *Manage Stakeholders Engagement*. But the foundation is laid in Project Initiation when we *Identify Stakeholders* (3.4.1) and in Project Planning when we *Collect Requirements* (3.4.2.1).

3.4.4   Monitoring and Controlling

In the processes of Monitoring and Controlling we track and review the performance of the project with regard to sustainability as well. These processes are indirectly impacted by principles of sustainability. The goals and purpose of the project are defined in Project Initiation. Requirements, budget and time frame are further defined in Project Planning. Project activities are then conducted in Project Execution and their performance is measured here in Monitoring and Controlling. Since we considered aspects of sustainability in scope, time, risk, cost, procurement and quality management, all of these aspects will be controlled and reviewed for fulfillment and performance here.

Specific methods or tools for sustainability can be applied in *Control Costs*. We can use the methods of *Eco-Accounting* described in section 4.3.

3.4.5   Closing

One of the purposes of the process *Close Project or Phase* is to provide lessons learned and to lead to a transition of the service or product of the project into operation. Handover and improvements through the application of principles of sustainability are a major concern of our efforts. This has been discussed in section 2.1 on the role of Program Management. That is the reason for us sustainable project managers to actually execute these activities at the end of the project life cycle. What we should do is to provide information about improvements in a before-after scenario. All of the methods of Three Steps to Sustainability can be used, i.e. *Checklists*, *Scoring System* and *Eco-Accounting*.

Lessons learned from this process will be used for the continuous improvement of these methods in your organization.

Knowledge Areas	Project Management Process Groups				
	Initiation	Planning	Executing	Monitoring/ Controlling	Closing
4. Project Integration Management	4.1 Develop Project Charter	4.2 Develop Project Management Plan	4.3 Direct and Manage Project Execution	4.4 Monitor and Control Project Work 4.5 Perform Integrated Change Control	4.6 Close Project or Phase
5. Project Scope Management		5.1 Plan Scope Management 5.2 Collect Requirements 5.3 Define Scope 5.4 Create WBS		5.5 Validate Scope 5.6 Control Scope	
6. Project Time Management		6.1 Plan Schedule Management 6.2 Define Activities 6.3 Sequence Activities 6.4 Estimate Activity Resources 6.5 Estimate Activity Durations 6.6 Develop Schedule		6.7 Control Schedule	
7. Project Cost Management		7.1 Plan Cost Management 7.2 Estimate Costs 7.3 Determine Budget		7.4 Control Costs	
8. Project Quality Management		8.1 Plan Quality Management	8.2 Perform Quality Assurance	8.3 Control Quality	
9. Project Human Resource Management		9.1 Develop Human Resource Plan	9.2 Acquire Project Team 9.3 Develop Project Team 9.4 Manage Project Team		
10. Project Communications Management		10.1 Plan Communications Management	10.2 Manage Communications	10.3 Control Communications	
11. Project Risk Management		11.1 Plan Risk Management 11.2 Identify Risks 11.3 Perform Qualitative Risk Analysis 11.4 Perform Quantitative Risk Analysis 11.5 Plan Risk Responses		11.6 Control Risks	
12. Project Procurement Management		12.1 Plan Procurement Management	12.2 Conduct Procurements	12.3 Control Procurements	12.4 Close Procurements
13. Project Stakeholder Management	13.1 Identify Stakeholders	13.2 Plan Stakeholder Management	13.3 Manage Stakeholders Engagement	13.4 Control Stakeholder Management	

Table 2: Process Groups for Sustainability

4. Three Steps to Sustainability

4.1 Checklists

4.1.1 Decision Making

The first step to sustainability in projects is the use of checklists. They contain criteria for exclusion, so-called *knock-outs* and criteria the project is obligated to meet, so-called *must-haves*. In case you check the former the project should not be executed. In case you check the latter only, then the project can be executed. Examples of knock-outs might be the production of toxic waste as a result of the project or a dependency on child labor. A *must-have* could be a reduction in CO_2 emission. If there is no reduction you might not want to execute that project.

Besides these knock-outs and must-haves we also use *desired effects* in the checklist. Examples are the use of trains instead of trucks or ships instead of planes for transportation. Another desired effect could be the reduction of noise in the office or on the production line. Checking the desired effects with our checklists can be helpful as a decision tool: when we have different projects or different approaches within a project we can then choose the alternative, which has more desired effects than the other.

Checklist Sustainable PM				
Project:	Sustainable Logistics			
	Type	knock-out 4	must 4	desirable 4
Planet				
Transport				
Train	desirable			x
Combined rail-truck transport	desirable			
Truck	desirable			
Euro-5	must			
Optimized aerodynamics	desirable			
Ship	desirable			
Plane	knock-out			
Routing optimization	must			
Combined product transportation	desirable			
Packaging				
Reduction	must			
Recyclable	desirable			
Toxic	knock-out			
Optimized warehousing	desirable			
Location				
Energy				
Emissions				
Eco-friendly coolant	must			
Noise reduction	desirable			
Waste				
Water				
People				
Labour Practice				
Accordance with local laws	must		x	
Accordance with home country standards	desirable			x
Accordance with international social standards	must		x	
Reduction of accidents at work	desirable			
Improvement in labour/management relations	desirable			

Figure 13: Checklist for Sustainability (Excerpt)

In many cases you will already have checklists in use during project initiation. This is a common method during the project initiation process for making decisions on which projects to choose or not. You can just add the sustainability criteria to your existing checklists. Thus you include the consequences of your project, which emerge in the mid term and long term perspective, into your decision process. This will enhance the project qualification process for the projects of your organization that are already in place.

4.1.2   Checklist Criteria

The checklist we use for *Three Steps to Sustainability* uses three dimensions with different categories on several levels. On the top level we have the three dimensions *planet, people* and *profit* derived from the Triple Bottom Line as described in 3.2.

4.1.2.1   Planet

What comes to mind first when we think about sustainability is *planet* representing our environment. For *planet* we have several categories that we check on: *transport, location, energy, emissions, waste, water* and *paper*. For the category *transport* we distinguish between *train, truck, ship* and *plane*, where in this case train, truck and ship are rated as *desirable* and plane is a knock-out criterion. In addition to these modes of transportation we have a couple of independent attributes like *routing optimization* and *optimized warehousing* For *location* it is important that it does not violate any protected areas, that it is close to sustainable transportation facilities and that it is optimized for the use of energy and resources. For *energy* we have the use of nuclear power sources as a knock-out criterion. Water power, solar power and fuel cells are rated as desirable. Natural gas and diesel engines are neutral and checked for documentation purposes. The use of biodiesel made from rapeseed is also a knock-out-criterion whereas biodiesel from used cooking oil is rated as desirable. In the category of emissions we have assessments for noise and gases harmful to the atmosphere like some coolants. For *waste* we have decomposable, recyclable, reusable as desirable attributes. Toxic wastes as an outcome of the project would be a knock-out (k.o.). In *water* and *paper* we are looking for ways of saving these resources and taking them to recycling or environmentally safe procedures of disposal.

4.1.2.2 People

While *planet* is on everybody's mind in the context of sustainability, *people* is the dimension that many project managers pay the least attention to. Environmental effects are more important e.g. for construction companies. If you are a working in the IT industry your project might have not so many measurable effects on the environment. It might also be that you are not so dependent on resources from developing countries or that you do not feel an outreach of your projects to your local community. For the most part in *IT projects* it is the team and the users of deliverables of the project who are most affected by it and responsible for the success of it. Therefore the wellbeing of these people is a major concern and should be central for responsible and sustainable project management. It is not just that a healthy team is more productive than a stressed and burnt-out one. It saves cost to have everybody on board instead of spending days on sick leave and therapy hours. Your team members will also readily be available for the next project when you need them. For the assessments of impacts on people it also helps to keep an eye on effects of your product on potential users. If it contributes to improvements of their situation at work or at home, your product will be more successful and it will cause less additional cost for maintenance and customer complaints.

But how can you manage a project team sustainably? In HR management we see many initiatives to train people on coping with the symptoms of stress. We find training courses on relaxation techniques and healthy thinking styles. During these sessions people are supposed to learn how to reduce the negative effects of work in order to manage stress and burn-out. However for sustainable projects we learned that it is better to avoid negative effects before they arise instead of dealing with their consequences. This can be done by increasing the positive effects and creating conditions in which you and your team can *flourish*. There are four strategies to achieve this flourishing (Silvius, Schipper, Planko, van den Brink, & Köhler, 2012):

The first strategy is to manage positive goals. This can be done by linking project goals to personal goals of the team members. Your project goals should also be challenging but achievable for the team. Anything else would be too boring or too stressful.

The second one is to manage positive emotions. Working on the creation of a positive but authentic professional atmosphere and paying attention to positive events during your projects and everyday work are the things to do here.

The third strategy is closely related to the fourth one. It is about managing positive relations. Positive language is the key for this strategy. An example of that is to tell a team member to come to work earlier and on time for her meetings, instead of talking about not being too late in order to avoid missing the start of a meeting.

The fourth strategy is to manage the strengths of people instead of their weaknesses. This approach challenges a major paradigm of classic project management, because it asks project managers to build the tasks in a project around the people instead of assigning people to already existing tasks. Its purpose is to lead the project team to the highest level of productivity possible. As a consequence the starting point for planning is not the work breakdown structure (WBS) as we were told in classic project management training. Planning should start with the assessment of strengths and the availability of your team members. This availability is checked during the process of *Acquire Project Team* and is documented in the project's *resource calendar*.

In order to achieve the flourishing team, these topics are included in our checklist for *people*.

4.1.2.3 Profit

For impacts of our projects on the dimension *profit* we check on topics like ROI, agility in business, communication, public relations and compliance. The complete checklist is available with a license for our method of sustainable project management supported by BibeZu at info@bibezu.de. Revenues from these licenses contribute to further research and projects of this non-profit organization.

An additional source for qualitative assessments of projects and business operations are the *Sustainability Reporting Guidelines* developed and published by the Global Reporting Initiative ™ (Global Reporting Initiative (TM), 2013). These guidelines provide you with categories and aspects of sustainability similar to the concept of the Triple Bottom Line.

4.2   Scoring System

The second step to sustainability after our project has passed the checklist test is a *qualitative assessment* using a scoring system. This scoring system uses the same categories as our checklists. Therefore we find the categories of the 3BL (Triple Bottom Line) at the top level and respective attributes below that.

In a first step every category is weighted against the other categories of the same level on a scale of 0 to 100%. The essential of our scoring system is that all weights of categories at the same level sum up to 100%. Lower levels also sum up to 100% each. After this weighting we score each attribute on a scale of 1 to 10, where a score of 10 is very positive and 1 is least positive with regard to the sustainability of the project.

			Assessment Sustainable PM		
			Project:	Logistics NewBread	
Sum of Weights 100%				Score	Weighted Score 5,2
30%	100%		Planet		1,4
	25%		Transport	5	1,3
			Train (10)		
			Truck (5)		
			Ship (7)		
			Plane (2)		
	25%		Energy	2	0,5
			Nuclear sources (1)		
			Water power (6)		
			Solar (9)		
			Natural gas (4)		
			Diesel engine (2)		
			Fuel cells (9)		
	20%		Waste	5	1,0
	30%		Water	6	1,8
30%	100%		People		1,8
	20%	100%	Labor Practice	30	1,5
	45%	100%	Human Rights	20	4,5
	35%	95%	Community Support	0	0
40%	100%		Profit		2
	50%		ROI	5	2,5
	50%		Agility in Business	5	2,5

Figure 14: Scoring for Sustainability

In that way we receive an overall score between 1 and 10 for the whole project. A score of 1 means that the project is quite negative with regard to sustainability. On the other hand a project with a score of 10 contributes very well to sustainability. Using these scores means that we decide between different projects on an *ordinal scale*. We can also compare different approaches for one project on the lower levels for each category.

In our example shown in *Figure 14: Scoring for Sustainability* we made the assessment for the dimension *planet* based on the four categories *transport, energy, waste* and *water*.

Transport received a weight of 25%, *energy* 25% also, *waste* has 20% and *water* 30% adding up to 100% within the category *planet*. *Transport* has several different instances like *train, truck, ship* and *plane*. These are rated according to their level of contribution to sustainability. In our example we chose a value of ten for *train*, five for transportation by *truck*, seven for *ship* and two for *plane*. These values are still subjective, of course, and very much dependent on the goals and circumstances of your company. But they allow for a more detailed comparison of alternative project approaches than the simple knock-outs, must-haves and desirables that we used in our checklist as a first step to sustainability.

In our example we use trucks for transportation. Therefore *transport* scores with a rounded 1.3 as a result of 5 times 25%. *Energy* scores 0.5, *waste* 1.0 and *water* 1.8. The sum of these scores for *planet* is 4.6. *Planet* itself has a weight of 30% in comparison to 30% for *people* and 40% for *profit*. Again these weights for the three dimensions of the Triple Bottom Line are subjective and specific to every company and organization.

4.6 for *planet* with a weight of 30% makes a rounded 1.4 contributing to the overall weighted score of 5.2 for the project. Remember that we were working on a scale from 1 to 10. So this project has a medium score for sustainability. It still has some potential for optimization. But on the other hand it does not seem to make things worse than before.

This scoring approach might seem quite similar to the use of a checklist in section *4.1*. However it takes more effort to conduct this qualitative assessment. It is better used to improve and optimize your project plan. Therefore it actually does make sense to use the checklists first in order to get a quick decision whether to proceed with initiating this project or not. Then you can go into more detail and score the project. Checklists are also recommendable for smaller budgets with less time for the project manager to spend on initiation.

The complete scoring sheet of our example is also available with a license for our method *Three Steps to Sustainability* at info@bibezu.de.

Once you are familiar with the scoring system and you have found all the attributes that contribute to sustainability, you will realize that it will show not so much potential for the optimization of your projects. That is due to the nature of qualitative assessments like our scoring on sustainability. Once you get to this point you should move on to a quantitative assessment. Quantitative measurements are easier to communicate to your stakeholders. For them it is easy to understand if you tell them that your project will save 500 tons of emissions of carbon dioxide into the atmosphere or € 120,000 in costs for waste disposal. It is harder for them to get a grip on the statement that your projects now score an average of 8.2 for sustainability by comparison with 3.8 five years ago. The next section *4.3 Eco-Accounting* will explain how such a quantitative assessment will be possible for your project.

4.3   Eco-Accounting

The next step to sustainability is to conduct an assessment on a cardinal scale. In this process you identify numerical values for the impacts of your project, which can then be used as a basis for calculation, just like measurements of length, volume or monetary values. This is something we are very familiar with. That makes it easy to communicate impacts and values to our stakeholders. Comparisons between different approaches for your sustainable project and even comparisons with competing conventional projects are possible on this level of assessment. There are different methods available for eco-accounting. One is to use so-called *Environmental Burden Points (EBPs)*.

The following section on EBPs might appear to be quite theoretical and abstract to you. However the principles described here are basic for many other methods of eco-accounting. Reading through this section will help you to get a grasp of these principles. This makes it easier to evaluate the applicability of any other method to your project or your organization. You will also be able to assess methods of other project managers inside and outside your organization. Later on with some experience in eco-accounting for project management you will adapt and optimize the methods you have been applying so far. So take the time to read and think through these descriptions for more success and sustainability in your projects.

The following sections 4.3.3 *Mandatory Carbon Reporting* and 4.3.6 *Monetary Values of CO2* also describe methods of eco-accounting with specific numbers and values that you may use for your projects.

4.3.1   Environmental Burden Points

Environmental Burden Points (EBPs) are calculated on the basis of *ecological scarcity*. This is the quotient of the so-called *actual flow* and the *critical flow* of a resource we use in a project (Braunschweig & Müller-Wenk, 1993, p. 46 ff.).

$$\text{Ecological Scarcity} = \frac{\text{Actual Flow}}{\text{Critical Flow}}$$

Critical flow is reached when the use of that specific resource starts impacting the environment. That critical flow is determined in environmental studies and available for many natural resources and emissions of production processes, as we will see later on. It is a fixed value and cannot be changed by any activities in your project.

What will be changed by your project is the actual flow. Your project contributes to the actual flow. That is represented in the EBP we are about to calculate here. The output of your project plus the actual flow already around in your area is then the actual impact on the environment. As actual flow is the nominator, and critical flow is the denominator for ecological scarcity. This means that the closer the actual flow or usage of a resource is to the critical usage, the higher is the value of its ecological scarcity.

This ecological scarcity is used to calculate the so-called *eco-factor*. Mathematically the eco-factor persists of the ecological scarcity of a certain resource multiplied with the inversion of the critical flow per year. This multiplication seems to be redundant. But it is done in order to receive the EBPs without a certain unit for measurement. That way we can aggregate EBPs for different resources into one measurement for the overall impact of our project.

$$\text{Eco Factor} = \frac{1}{\text{Critical Flow}} \times \frac{\text{Actual Flow}}{\text{Critical Flow}}$$

Our example equation shows that for an impact like the emission of carbon dioxide measured in tons per year (ton/a) we receive an eco-factor with a dimension of *year per ton* (a/ton). How this is related to the EBPs will be shown in the next equation, where we actually calculate them.

$$\text{Eco Factor} = \frac{1}{\frac{\text{ton}}{a}} \times \frac{\text{ton}}{\text{ton}} = \frac{a \times \text{ton}}{\text{ton}^2} = \frac{a}{\text{ton}}$$

This eco-factor in a/ton is multiplied with the output of your project in ton/a for instance. The numbers you receive do not have a unit of measurement. Therefore impacts of different sources with different measures can be aggregated into one total impact for the entire project.

Eco-factors are usually calculated by environmental assessment organizations such as the BUWAL in Switzerland. BUWAL is the abbreviation for "Bundesamt für Umwelt, Wald und Landwirtschaft", which means federal authority on environment, woods and agriculture. Eco-factors from BUWAL and others are multiplied with a *scaling factor* in order to receive numbers that are easier to handle. In this case the scaling factor is 10^9.

Now that we have the eco-factor and the current flow of a resource or emission induced by our project, we can finally calculate the EBPs. For example emissions of sulfur dioxide in Switzerland have an eco-factor of 23,000 EBP/kg SO_2 /year. Let us assume we have a current emission of 10 kg as an impact of our project. That would then result in 230,000 EBPs as you can see in Table 3: *Calculation of EBP*.

We can combine these EBPs of sulfur dioxide with EBPs calculated for the impact of nitrogen oxide released by our sample project. For nitrogen oxide we have an eco-factor of 42,300 EBP/kg NOx /year. Multiplied with 5 kg from our project we get 211,500 EBPs for these emissions and can aggregate them to 441,500 EBPs for sulfur dioxide and nitrogen dioxide together.

Impact	X	Eco-factor	=	EBP
10 kg SO_2 / a	x	23 000 EBP / kg SO_2 /a	=	230,000 EBP
5 kg NOx / a	x	42 300 EBP / kg NOx / a	=	211,500 EBP
Impact on planet			=	441,500 EBP

Table 3: Calculation of EBP
(Braunschweig & Müller-Wenk, 1993, p. 48)

Once the EBPs for different factors have been determined, they can be used to aggregate the impacts of different factors such as noise, land usage and emissions of carbon dioxide just as we can aggregate the value of different goods like apples and pears by using their prices on the market or their weights in kilograms.

EBPs can also be used to calculate trade-offs between different impacts. For instance is it worthwhile to save 2 kg of NOx if we generate 3 kg more of SO_2? Yes, it is, because the sum of EBPs is lower than it was before, as you can see in Table 4: *Trade-offs with EBPs*.

Impact	X	Eco-factor	=	EBP
13 kg SO_2 / a	x	23,000 EBP / kg SO_2 /a	=	299,000 EBP
3 kg NOx / a	x	42,300 EBP / kg NOx / a	=	126,900 EBP
Impact on planet			=	425,900 EBP

Table 4: Trade-offs with EBPs

EBPs for different resources or types of emissions in different countries are not always easily available. In many cases this may be the major obstacle for project managers wishing to achieve this last level of measuring sustainability. However for impacts on *planet* you might refer to environmental authorities of your country or region. You can focus on major impacts where data about critical and actual flow is available.

For impacts on *people* you might refer to data provided by local health and labor ministries, health insurances or social welfare organizations. For instance you can look at figures of how many hours of overtime per month people can endure before sickness or turnover rates rise. This will then be your critical flow. Then you can check what the actual average hours of overtime are in your organization. That will be your actual flow. You can then calculate the *eco-factors for hours of overtime*.

For instance if you find out that 10 hours is critical and 5 hours is the actual flow in your organization, you will get an eco-factor of 50,000,000. So every hour of overtime that is added to the people working on your project or reduced for staff affected by your project has this value of 50,000,000. And now it can even be compared to a reduction of SO_2. One hour of overtime so to speak needs a reduction of 2,174 kg of SO_2 to be compensated. This might seem to be a strange comparison to you. But it shows how trade-offs in projects could be made in order to arrive at a holistic assessment of its impacts.

Actually that is what many companies are doing with monetary values. They compare costs of labor with costs of machinery in euros or US dollars. But as we have learned, these monetary values do not include the costs of external effects and cannot be applied for purposes of sustainability. Of course they can be used to assess the costs of investing in sustainability. And then we – as sustainable project managers – in many cases cannot answer the question how these costs are related to monetary improvements for our organizations, which are the impacts on profits. However, we learned how to communicate these improvements on an ordinal scale with qualitative arguments in section 4.2 *Scoring System*. And we will see how we can develop monetary values for these improvements in section 4.3.6 *Monetary Values of CO_2*.

One example of the identification of EBPs for *planet* is the work of the *Intergovernmental Panel on Climate Change (IPCC)*. In order to estimate the effects of emissions of different greenhouse gases the researchers have calculated *CO_2 equivalents*(CO_2-EQ), which they call *Global Warming Potential* (GWP). Table 2.14 of this report shows the GWPs for many different greenhouse gases (IPCC, 2007b, p. 212). Our *Table 5: CO_2 Equivalents of Greenhouse Gases* shows values for the best known greenhouse gases CO_2, methane and nitrous oxide.

Greenhouse Gas	GWP (in kg CO_2-EQ/kg)
Carbon dioxide (CO_2)	1
Methane (CH_4)	21
HFC-23 (CHF_3)	11,700
Nitrous oxide (N_2O)	310
PFC-14 (CF_4)	6,500
Sulfur hexafluoride (SF_6)	23,900
	(IPCC, 2007a, p. 212), Section 2, Table 2.14

Table 5: CO_2 Equivalents of Greenhouse Gases

These numbers have been used in the German *Report on the Potential of the Waste Industry to Protect the Climate* (Dehoust, Schüler, Vogt, & Giegrich, 2010) in order to come up with aggregated numbers for pollution, emissions, savings and trade-offs for different treatment scenarios. GWPs can help you in your organization to report on impacts on *planet*. You can aggregate different environmental factors and of course you can also compare different scenarios and calculate trade-offs.

The results and the concept of IPCC for CO_2-EQs are also the basis for the methods described in the following sections.

4.3.2　Ecological Footprint

The concept of critical flow is used by the *Global Footprint Network* (GFN), an association focused on the calculation of sustainable emissions of carbon dioxide. In their concept the critical flow is called *biocapacity*. The measurement for it is *global hectares* (gha). It is the capacity of an ecosystem to produce useful biological materials. Useful here means that it serves the demands of human society. *Biocapacity* also includes the ability to absorb waste materials generated by human activities such as CO_2 in a given year (Global Footprint Network, 2013b). GFN publishes data for many countries for current and historic footprints. For example in Germany there is a biocapacity of about 2 global hectares (gha) per capita. The actual ecological footprint is more than 4 gha with a slight trend downwards.

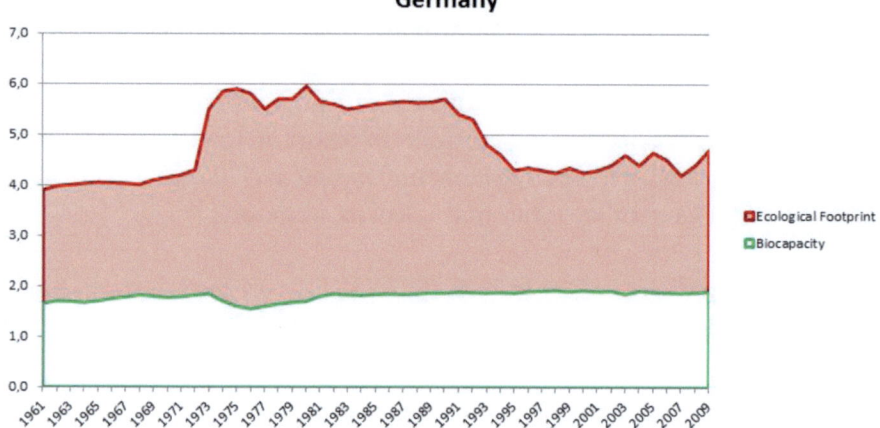

©2003-2013 Global Footprint Network
Figure 15: Ecological Footprint for Germany

In comparison Cameroon also had a biocapacity of 2 gha per capita in 2009. However it has steadily been dropping to this level from 6 gha in 1961. Biocapacity according to GFN is not a constant for every year. It varies with agricultural practices, weather and population size. In this case the latter will be the reason for the decreasing values of biocapacity, since Cameroon has experienced an extensive growth in population from a level of 5 million people in 1961 to more than 20 million in 2013 (Wikipedia, 2013a).

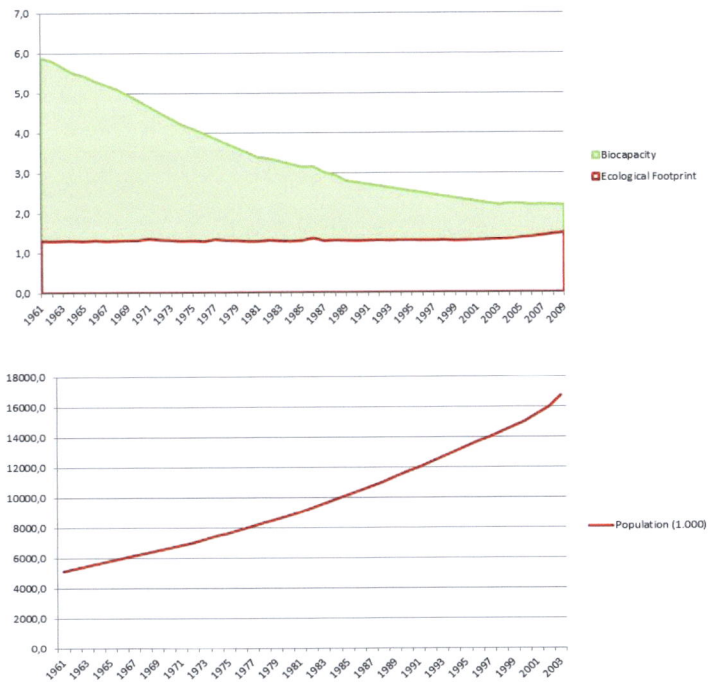

©2003-2013 Global Footprint Network, Wikipedia, 2013a
Figure 16: Biocapacity and Population of Cameroon

Given the fact that we expect a growing population worldwide, it is clear that there will be a major trend of diminishing biocapacity on the global level as well. For the wellbeing of our planet the ecological footprints of China and India will be decisive, since we have about a third of the world's population in these countries. Unfortunately there has been a strong negative trend for the footprint of China in the last 10 years. As we can see in Figure 17: *Ecological Footprint of China* the biocapacity of China has remained steadily on a level of about 1 gha per capita. But the footprint has steeply gone up from 1.5 to a level of 2.4 gha within the last 10 years. This is still less than 4 gha in Germany but the divergence still seems to be growing rapidly.

71

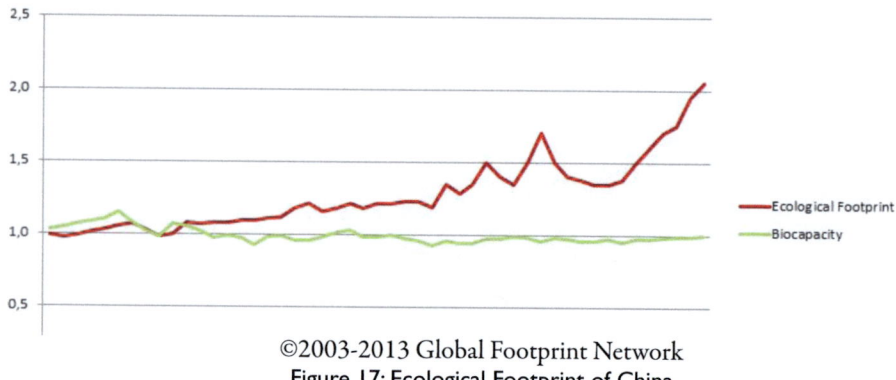

Figure 17: Ecological Footprint of China

These figures were a slight deviation from the topic of eco-accounting in projects. But they will enhance your motivation for working on improvements in sustainability and they show a method for combining effects of different processes and materials in one quantity. As a project manager you can use this figures to set the goals of your organization for the reduction of emissions in carbon dioxide. For a German enterprise the goal has to be to cut emissions by 50% in order to be sustainable, similar in China. In Cameroon that value would be 25%.

4.3.3 Mandatory Carbon Reporting

In 2013 the UK government became the first country to introduce compulsory reporting on emissions of all six so-called Kyoto greenhouse gases including CO_2, CH_4, N_2O, HFCs, PFCs and SF_6. It is based on the *Companies Act 2006 (Strategic Report and Directors' Report) Regulations 2013* (HM Government, UK, 2013) and is called *Mandatory Carbon Reporting*. It applies to all UK incorporated companies listed on the main market of the London Stock Exchange, the New York Stock Exchange or NASDAQ. Even if your company may not be listed on the stock exchange, it may be a supplier to one of these companies and therefore also affected by this law. Since carbon reporting includes the supply chain of a company, your customer might be entitled to insist that you provide him with data about the carbon footprint of the goods and services that you deliver to him. This is driving many companies that have not been thinking about sustainability in the past to do so now by regulation.

The Department for Environment, Food and Rural Affairs (DEFRA) supplies powerful tools for measuring and reporting CO_2 equivalents (CO_2-EQs) on its website (Department for Environment, Food and Rural Affairs, 2013a). It even provides a comprehensive collection of greenhouse gas conversion factors. They have been developed for use in annual business reports and are very well applicable to projects as well (Department for Environment, Food and Rural Affairs, 2013c). From my point of view this is currently the ultimate tool for you to use for assessments and communications on sustainability in your projects. Figure 18 shows an extract from the tables provided.

What's new?

Where a vehicle is used by an organisation but isn't owned by them, these vehicles can be reported in scope 3 instead of scope 1, using the same factors. (These factors can also be found in the scope 3 under 'business travel-land' or 'managed assets- vehicles').

Activity	Type	Unit	Diesel				Petrol				Unknown			
			kg CO₂e	kg CO₂	kg CH₄	kg N₂O	kg CO₂e	kg CO₂	kg CH₄	kg N₂O	kg CO₂e	kg CO₂	kg CH₄	kg N₂O
Cars (by size)	Small car	km	0,14048	0,13866	0,00005	0,00177	0,16192	0,16122	0,00014	0,00056	0,15557	0,15458	0,00011	0,00088
		miles	0,226081	0,223152	0,00008	0,002849	0,260585	0,259458	0,000225	0,000901	0,250366	0,248772	0,000177	0,001416
	Medium car	km	0,12475	0,17293	0,00005	0,00177	0,2049	0,2042	0,00014	0,00056	0,19083	0,18967	0,0001	0,00106
		miles	0,281233	0,278304	0,00008	0,002849	0,329755	0,328628	0,000225	0,000901	0,307111	0,305244	0,000161	0,001706
	Large car	km	0,22941	0,22759	0,00005	0,00177	0,29678	0,29608	0,00014	0,00056	0,25023	0,24885	0,00008	0,0013
		miles	0,3692	0,366271	0,00008	0,002849	0,477621	0,476495	0,000225	0,000901	0,402706	0,400485	0,000129	0,002092
	Average car	km	0,18322	0,1814	0,00005	0,00177	0,19811	0,19741	0,00014	0,00056	0,19023	0,18908	0,0001	0,00105
		miles	0,294864	0,291935	0,00008	0,002849	0,318827	0,317701	0,000225	0,000901	0,306146	0,304295	0,000161	0,00169

FAQs

Do the conversion factors take into account the age of vehicles?

The conversion factors are based on information from the DfT (Department for Transport) who regularly analyse the mix of cars on the road in Britain through DVLA records and automatic number plate recognition (ANPR) data. The conversion factors are updated each year to reflect changes in the spectrum of cars of different types and ages being driven.

I know the average mpg of my passenger vehicles as well as mileage; can this be used to improve my calculations?

The mpg (miles per gallon) of the vehicle should be used to convert the distance travelled into litres of fuel used (refer to the 'conversions' listing to find values to assist this calculation). The conversion factor for litres of fuel can then be applied, which will give a more accurate view of the actual emissions from the vehicle (the conversion factors for vehicle mileage represent the average mpg of the whole UK vehicle population, therefore knowing your vehicle's actual mpg and using this value will yield more precise results).

I know the average gCO₂/km of my passenger vehicles as well as mileage; can this be used to improve my calculations?

If you know the manufacturers gCO₂/km data this may be used as an alternative (and more precise) calculation for your passenger vehicle's emissions. The factors provided by manufacturers should be uplifted by 15% and multiplied by the km distance travelled in the vehicle.

Figure 18: DEFRA CO₂ Conversion Factors 2012

These factors are made for UK companies. However I found them to be very well applicable to international companies as well. Unless you have better figures available in your region, the DEFRA conversion factors will come as close to the real ones as you can get. At least all these factors have been identified on a common data basis. And our major goal here is to be able to compare different categories with each other in order to compare and improve our activities towards more sustainability. DEFRA also provides a guideline on how to apply their factors to SMEs (Department for Environment, Food and Rural Affairs, 2013b). It can provide rapid help for applying these factors to your organization.

There are other tools available that can help you to compile and report your greenhouse gas emissions. There is the *CarbonNeutral Footprint Reporter* (The CarbonNeutral Company Limited, 2013a) or the CO_2-*compensation* tools from atmosfair (atmosfair gGmbH, 2013). They can be used in individual projects as well as for the whole organization. Once you know the amount of CO_2-equivalents induced by your project, company or organization during a certain time period you can then buy compensation certificates for this amount and receive a CO_2-*free project* or company.

This might seem too easy for some of you and some might even call it *greenwashing*. I think it is one step on the long road to sustainability. It creates awareness of impacts on the Triple Bottom Line (3BL) caused by our economic activities. It makes these impacts quantifiable, which gives us an opportunity to communicate improvements and successes of our projects. It is based on monetary values for impacts on 3BL, which provides us with arguments in discussions about investments and business cases with our project sponsors. Finally the compensation contributions are used for projects that help to avoid, reduce or compensate CO_2 emissions by building power plants based on renewable energies, reforestation, or promoting technologies for efficient cooking in developing countries. This helps to build the sustainable economic infrastructure that we all need so urgently for a real prosperous future.

4.3.4   Impacts on Profit

Impacts on *profit* are very easy to assess. This is the dimension that we are used to calculating in numbers, i.e. prices and figures of currency. Usually there are higher costs for sustainable projects because investments in new technologies or processes have to be made, compensations for CO_2 emissions are paid, staff have to be trained, communication processes will be changed and so on.

On the other hand when following sustainable principles most companies experience a decrease of costs due to lower turnover and sickness rates with their staff, savings in energy and resource consumption, and lower bills for waste treatment. And they experience an increase in customer loyalty, acceptance of higher prices due to an improved perception of quality for their products and services, improved recognition and higher turnover in ecologically sensitive customer segments (Canella, 2007). Overall sustainability causes investment but tends to create a good business and has positive impacts on profits.

4.3.5   Impacts on People

Regarding the impacts on people in eco-accounting it is best to start by looking at the staff in your own organization before looking at the global population. It might take some research in your organization, but usually you will quickly be able to calculate costs of sick leave and reduced productivity of your staff. The approach is to calculate an average hourly or daily cost rate of your employees. Then you find out the number of days people currently stay away from the company due to stressful or unhealthy working conditions. Multiplying this number by the average cost rate gives you the current costs of sick leave in your company.

Finally you make an assessment of the number of days that can be reduced due to improvements in noise emission and working atmosphere, cleaner air and better lighting in offices or on the production line, enhanced flexibility of working hours and so on. This is also multiplied by the average cost rate and shows the value for your sustainable project management approach.

In addition to these costs for sick leave or employee fluctuation, you will be able to identify costs of medication and treatment for people suffering from certain diseases. These numbers can be provided by your local health insurance organization For example we know that there are costs of €35 billion per year in Germany and €126 billion in the European Union (EU) for the treatment of cancer patients (Frankfurter Allgemeine Zeitung, 2013). If you believe that environmental pollution, bad nutrition and an unhealthy working atmosphere contribute to human disease, you may include these figures in the eco-accounting of your project. Positive or negative effects can be determined by making assumptions for improvements or deteriorations of these factors quantified in a fraction or percentage. That is an example of the effects we can have on the dimension *people* on the level of your organization, society and the national economy.

4.3.6 Monetary Values of CO_2

From assessments on profit and people we switch back to effects of your projects on *planet*. In our day the accumulation of carbon dioxide (CO_2) in the atmosphere is the most widely public and globally discussed effect of our behavior on planet. Therefore a lot of scientific organizations have been calculating EBPs for CO_2. The EBPs in this case are even available in currency units of euros or US dollars per kilogram. E.g. for their system of emission trading the United States have set a price of 13 US dollars or about 10 euros per ton of carbon dioxide (Ziener & Rinke, 2009). In addition figures and tables for the emission of CO_2 are widely available for many resources, especially for the usage of means of transportation like cars, trains or airplanes.

There is a widely accepted assumption that the emission of 3000 kg of CO_2 per capita per year is the limit for not causing atmospheric changes leading to global warming. This would be our critical flow.[1] On this basis different institutions have calculated the monetary value for emitting one kg of CO_2. Examples are shown in Figure 19: *Calculations of Ecological Impact on a Cardinal Scale.* Most of the results we found are between €0.06 and €0.07 per kg of CO_2. This is a number that you can use when comparing different alternatives for your project.

For example you can compare the assignment of a project manager for a project in Munich, Germany. There is one candidate who is living in Hamburg and would be flying once a week from there to the project site in Munich and back home at the end of the week. The plane ticket for one round trip in the economy class causes 330 kg of CO_2 for 1300 km by plane and additional ecological costs of €23.1. For a working week with 40 hours this results in 8.25 kg CO_2 and €0.58 per hour of additional costs with regard to sustainability for this project manager.

As an alternative, there is another candidate who is living in a town 50 km south of Munich. She would commute to the project site by car every day. 100 km per day by car with an energy optimized Toyota Prius plug-in hybrid results in the release of 4.9 kg of CO_2. That means 0.61 kg CO_2 per hour for an eight hour working day or €0.043 per hour of additional costs. With respect to sustainability it would be better to appoint the project manager commuting with her car. In order to optimize the sustainability factor, it would even be better to pay for a hotel or introduce incentives for the project manager to travel by train. 100 km by

1   The average release of CO_2 per capita in Europe is 8 tons, in Germany 11 and in the USA 22 (Engel, 2011)

train every day result in the emission of 3.97 kg CO_2 and €0.035 per hour. This is even less than traveling by car. Going by train also has positive effects on *people* and *profits*. There is less risk of accidents. Traveling time can be used for reading and writing e-mails, preparation for meetings or just relaxation.

The price for CO_2 can also be used for calculations of the ecological value of your project. You do this by assessing the savings which will be achieved in the reductions of CO_2 emissions as a result of the way you organize your project.

Calculations

Emissions from trains of Deutsche Bahn

100 km resulting in 3.97 kg CO_2

Pricing according to *atmosfair*:

ecological costs per	100 km:	0.28 €

Emissions from an energy optimized car (Toyota Prius):

100 km resulting in 4.9 kg CO_2

ecological costs per	100 km:	€ 0,34

Emissions from a large car (VW Touareg):

100 km resulting 31.7 kg CO_2

ecological costs per	100km:	€ 2,24

Figure 19: Calculations of Ecological Impact on a Cardinal Scale

One very good example of eco-accounting in the production of clothing is the web site of Bruno Pieters for his prêt-à-porter collection *honest by*. Mr. Pieters wants to offer complete transparency of the related production processes. Therefore he documents where the materials for his clothes come from, how and where they are manufactured and the carbon footprint of each model. For example the production of one piece of his *Navy blue unisex organic denim bomber jacket with tweed sleeves* results in the release of 3.03 kg CO_2 which is the equivalent of driving a car for 18.04 km (Honest By, 2013).

4.3.7 Valuation Techniques

The previous section about monetary values of carbon dioxide emissions describes one example of transferring qualitative impacts on the Triple Bottom Line into quantitative figures. Maybe you are working in projects where CO_2 emissions do not appear to have a relevant impact, like in IT or HR development projects. However you see that your projects do have other important impacts on 3BL and you want to assess these impacts on the basis of monetary values.

There are many different industries with many different aspects of projects around the world. Many of them have their specific considerations on monetary values. There are a couple of methods for the valuation of these aspects and impacts. (University of Cambridge Programme for Sustainability Leadership, 2013, p. 66). Table 6: *Valuation Techniques* shows an overview of these methods. Some of them, like the *travel cost method* and the *hedonic pricing method*, are methods of indirect and analogous value estimation. Others, like *contingent valuation* and *market prices,* are aimed at determining ecological value directly through questionnaires and existing prices. All of them are based on the principle of human welfare. That means that we make a sophisticated guess at what people would be ready to pay for not being affected by impacts, or for the repair of the results in order to achieve, maintain or even improve the situation as it was before.

You may use these methods for the quantitative assessment of your projects with regard to sustainability whenever you are missing other appropriate measures. By that way you can develop your own set of KPIs and integrate them into the organizational process assets specific to your industry and company. I would be happy if you shared your experience with me, so that we can further develop our methodology for sustainable projects. Please feel free to contact me at sustainability@bibezu.de .

In case it is too costly or complicated for you to conduct your own studies for your specific organization, it is appropriate to use the outputs of previously conducted studies where available and suitable for your situation. This is a so-called *benefits transfer*. In order to work as exactly as possible, it is useful to choose between the four approaches to transfer described below (University of Cambridge Programme for Sustainability Leadership, 2013, p. 68).

4.3.7.1 Mean Value Transfer

In this first approach you use the mean values of the study site for your specific project site without adjustments. This works quite well when the study site and your project site are very similar, of course. In other cases you should try one of the following methods with adjustments.

4.3.7.2 Adjusted Value Transfer

This approach also uses the mean values from the study site, but they are adjusted for differences in specific characteristics like income of the population or currency values. This approach is suitable for use when characteristics of the study are known and differences to your project are measurable.

4.3.7.3 Value Function Transfer

In this case the economic model of the study is known and is then applied to your project site. This can be useful when you have statistical data available for a project e.g. from a national census or official statistical organizations. In any other case this is just like a specific study we described at the beginning of this section.

4.3.7.4 Meta-analytical Value Transfer

This is similar to the Value Function Transfer in that it is based on the model from a previous study, which is then applied to another project. In our case this other project could be yours. However in this approach you need quite a similar situation, and you are using not only the economic model but also known parameters like costs per hectare from the study for your project. Therefore one should be quite careful in applying this method of transfer.

4.4   Conclusion

The previous sections describing methods for the *Three Steps to Sustainability* provide you with powerful tools to incorporate the goals of sustainability in the projects of your organization. Ranging from simple and basic assessments like the checklist method to the complicated approaches for eco-accounting, you have the chance to start with the easy things and pick the low hanging fruits first. Once you have gained your first successes you can improve your organization with the help of the quantitative method of the scoring system. In the end you will finally reach the stage where sustainability becomes a natural aspect of everything you do. This is the point where quantitative assessments of eco-accounting will be used and will become part of your everyday work. For the sake of your personal future and the prosperity of our global community I wish you all the best, good luck and major successes on your way to sustainability. The following section 5 has some tips for where and how to obtain support on this path.

METHOD	DESCRIPTION
Travel cost method	Indirect estimation of demand, i.e. the willingness to pay by using travel costs actually paid to visit a site
Hedonic pricing method	Indirect estimation of willingness to pay using property price changes related to changes in the environment.
Contingent valuation	Direct survey-based estimation with hypothetical questions about willingness to pay to obtain more or less of an environmental good
Choice experiments	Direct survey-based estimation with hypothetical questions about willingness to pay to obtain more or less of an environmental good
Net Factor income, productivity method	Value assignment based on the revenue of an associated product's net costs of other inputs
Market prices	Direct measurement based on market prices for traded environmental goods
Replacement cost	Costs of replacing a natural function with an alternative, manmade technology or restoration of the ecosystem
Defensive expenditure method	Costs and expenditure incurred in avoiding damages of reduced environmental functionality

Table 6: Valuation Techniques

WELFARE ASPECTS	EXAMPLE
Recreational benefits of environmental settings and biodiversity	Assessing value of a forest that is supposed to become a site for a shopping mall and used to be a recreational site: count people visiting the site and draw a sample to figure out what costs they had to get there
Value of living in a certain environmental setting reflected in property prices	Comparison of prices for houses and land with similar size in a city between sites close to a highway and in quiet sites close to a recreational area
All welfare categories including biodiversity, human health, use values like recreation and non-use values like esthetics	Conducting a survey about the potential entrance fee to a nature park or parking fees close to it.
All welfare categories including biodiversity, human health, use values like recreation and non-use values like esthetics	Similar to contingent valuation above with closed instead of open questions, i.e. multiple choices of different prices.
Natural resources (water, land, soil, biodiversity, landscape) used to offer products	Analyzing financial statement of local water supply company for income based on provision of potable water
Crops, timber, fish, climate change, etc.	Measuring turnover from potential timber harvest in a natural reserve; turnover of restaurants in a scenic site
Human health, water treatment, pest and disease control	Costs of stress measured by cost of coronal surgery for a heart pacemaker or treatment after a heart attack
Storm and flood defense, erosion control, air quality impacts on human health	20 billion US dollars plan of City of New York to strengthen the city against flood damages

(University of Cambridge Programme for Sustainability Leadership, 2013, p. 66)

5   Community of Practice for Sustainable Development

In many cases sustainable project managers are like lone rangers on a dusty road to new horizons. It is not easy to convince your management, your team or your customers that there is a need for change. When times are getting tough and matters are getting rougher, you might even lose your own conviction. You will be tempted to switch back to the old and easier way of doing your project.

In that case you might think about Barack Obama's slogan "Yes, we can" or sing along with Jon Bon Jovi "Oh yes, we can". However the former is not a project manager but a politician, whose successes are questionable. And the latter is a musician. So they might not be able to provide you with the proper support. It might be a better choice for you to team up with other experienced project managers with the same goal of implementing sustainable practices in their projects.

The Project Management Institute (PMI®) is a global organization of project managers from all kinds of industries. It develops various standards and issues certifications for project managers at different levels. Beyond that it organizes so-called Communities of Practice (CoP). There is a growing CoP, which develops, discusses and promotes tools and methods for sustainability in project management. The so-called PMI® Global Sustainability Community of Practice is a platform for all interested project managers to exchange ideas in blogs and documents while keeping each other updated on the latest developments in sustainable project management.

For that purpose it issues newsletters and organizes regular webinars where presenters have an opportunity to talk about their experiences to a global audience. Especially the webinars are subject to a growing interest and are overbooked most of the time.

Those of you who are looking for support in sustainable project management may subscribe to the community at http://sustainability.vc.pmi.org/ (for registered users of pmi.org).

6   Numbers and Measures

6.1   Carbon Dioxide

Critical Flow	• 3000 kg / a per capita	(atmosfair gGmbH, 2013)

Monetary Value	• €0.06 per kg/ CO_2 • €0.07 €per kg/ CO_2 • $0.08 per kg/ CO_2	(atmosfair gGmbH, 2013) (Weindl, 2008) (University of Cambridge Programme for Sustainability Leadership, 2013)

Origin	Emissions	Source
Cars Germany	• 2.34 t CO_2/year ○ equivalent of 13,000 km/ year at <u>180 g CO_2/km</u> • 2 t CO_2/year at 12,000 km/ year	(Dehoust, Schüler, Vogt, & Giegrich, 2010) (atmosfair gGmbH, 2013)
Train Germany	• 2.9 l gas equivalent/ 100 km • <u>39.7 g CO_2/km and person</u> • 23.7 g CO_2/km per ton freight	(Verkehrsclub Deutschland e.V., 2007) (Deutsche Bahn AG, 2013b, p. 127)
Ships	• 11.5 g CO_2/km per ton freight	(Deutsche Bahn AG, 2013b, p. 127)
Planes	• 2.57 kg CO_2/l kerosene • 281.79 g CO_2/km per person • €0.0065/ km • 643 g CO_2/km per ton air-freight	(Hartmann & Wüpper, 2011) (atmosfair gGmbH, 2013) (Deutsche Bahn AG, 2013b, p. 127)

Electricity		
Germany:	0.598 kg CO_2/kWh (energy mix Germany)	(Dehoust, Schüler, Vogt, & Giegrich, 2010)
	Energy Mix Germany: 0.522 kg CO_2/kWh 0.0005 g radioactive waste/ kWh Energy Mix Dresden: 0.440 kg CO_2/kWh 0.0002 g radioactive waste/ kWh 0.2519 €/kWh Energy Mix "Electricity Nature" Dresden: 0 kg CO_2/kWh 0 g radioactive waste/ kWh 0.2543 €/kWh	(DREWAG, 2012)
	Energy Mix Munich: 0.305 kg CO_2/kWh 0.0001 g radioactive waste/ kWh 0.2531 €/kWh Energy Mix "M- Eco-Electricity": 0 kg CO_2/kWh 0 g radioactive waste/ kWh 0.2692 €/kWh	(Stadtwerke München GmbH, 2012)
USA	1.645 kg CO_2/kWh	(Logicalis U.S., 2013)
Refrigerator	100 kg CO_2/ a	(atmosfair gGmbH, 2013)

IT	• 2% of CO_2 emissions are caused by IT	(Merschmann, 2008)
	○ equal to all emissions of global air traffic.	
	• Notebook with 100W 60 g CO_2 per hour (Germany)	
	• PC with 1,314 kWh/a:	(Logicalis U.S., 2013)
	○ 1,760 kg CO_2/a (U.S.)	
	○ 785 kg CO_2/a (Germany)	
	○ Production consumes 535 kWh	(Arndt, Bormann, & Zehle, 2007, p. 23)
Google	• Google consumes 55 GWh of electricity per year	(Merschmann, 2008)
	○ equal to the annual consumption of electricity of a town with 45,000 inhabitants	
	○ equal to 33,000 t CO_2 (with 0.6 kg CO_2 per KWh or 600 kg per MWh)	
	○ one search request consumes 8 Wh, equal to 4.8 g CO_2	

6.2   Green IT

Energy budget	Portion of the IT-Budget for electricity • 20% for small data centers • 80% for large hosting providers	(Microsoft Corp., 2009)
Potential savings	• 15-25% by using Energy Star standard hardware • 80% by virtualization	(Microsoft Corp., 2009) (Binary Artworks, 2013)

6.3   Calorific Values

Wood pellets	• 4.9 kWh/kg
Heating oil	• 9.44 kWh/kg
Natural gas	• ~10 kWh/cbm

(Wikipedia, 2013b)

7 Table of Figures

8 Table of Tables

9 Bibliography

Arndt, L., Bormann, S., & Zehle, p. (2007). *Unsichtbare Kosten. Ungleiche Verteilung ökologischer Risiken in der globalen Computerindustrie.* Bonn: Weltwirtschaft Ökologie & Entwicklung e.V.

atmosfair gGmbH. (2013). *Meinen Flug kompensieren.* Retrieved December 02, 2013, from www.atmosfair.de: https://www.atmosfair.de/projekt2/flugrechner/

Belyakov, A., & Esakin, T. (2013, February 21). *A "Triple Bottom Line", Sustainability Project Evaluation Met.* Retrieved February 28, 2013, from PMI Gobal Sustainability Community Of Practice: http://sustainability.vc.pmi.org/Webinars/ViewWebinar.aspx?WebinarAction=View&WebinarExternalKey=b5dd3943-bad2-4297-9ef3-2f3fe78eaf87

Binary Artworks. (2013). *Cloud Computing im Mittelstand.* Braunschweig: Binary Artworks.

Braunschweig, A., & Müller-Wenk, R. (1993). *Ökobilanzen für Unternehmungen.* Stuttgart: Haupt.

Canella, C. (2007). Sustainability - A Green Formula. *2008 Leadership in Project Management*, pp. 34-40.

Carbon Footprint Ltd. (2013). *Mandatory Greenhouse Gas (GHG) Reporting.* Retrieved December 06, 2013, from Carbon Footprint: http://www.carbonfootprint.com/mandatorycarbonreporting.html

Carboni, J. (2013). *Sustainability in PM - Methods & Tools for Success.*
    Newtown Square: PMI.

Dehoust, G., Schüler, D., Vogt, R., & Giegrich, J. (2010).
    Klimaschutzpotenziale in der Abfallwirtschaft. Darmstadt,
    Heidelberg: Öko Institut e.V., ifeu Institut für Energie- und
    Umweltforschung.

Deland, D. (2009). Sustainability Through Project Management and
    Net Impact. *PMI Global Proceedings* (pp. 1-20). Orlando:
    Project Management Institute.

Department for Environment, Food and Rural Affairs. (2013a).
    *Measuring and reporting environmental impacts: guidance for
    businesses.* Retrieved December 06, 2013, from GOV.UK:
    https://www.gov.uk/measuring-and-reporting-environmental-
    impacts-guidance-for-businesses

Department for Environment, Food and Rural Affairs. (2013b).
    *SMALL BUSINESS USER GUIDE: Guidance on how to
    measure and report your greenhouse gas emissions.* London:
    Department for Environment, Food and Rural Affairs.

Department for Environment, Food and Rural Affairs. (2013c).
    Government conversion factors for company reporting. Retrieved
    December 06, 2013, from Greenhouse Gas Conversion Factor
    Repository: http://www.ukconversionfactorscarbonsmart.co.uk/

Deutsche Bahn AG. (2012). *www.bahn.de.* Retrieved from http://www.
    bahn.de

Deutsche Bahn AG. (2013a). Das wird eine Revolution. *mobil 10.2013,*
    10-14.

Deutsche Bahn AG. (2013b). *Nachhaltigkeitsbericht 2012*. Berlin: Deutsche Bahn AG.

Dohmen, C. (2013, May 17). Der kleine Unterschied. *Süddeutsche Zeitung*, p. 18.

DREWAG. (2012). *Stromkennzeichnung der DREWAG - Stadtwerke Dresden GmbH*. Retrieved November 19, 2013, from DREWAG Alles da. Alles nah. Alles klar.: http://www.drewag. de/de/privatkunden/drewag_produkte/strom/pk_dp_strom_ stromkennzeichnung.php

Eid, M. (2009). *Sustainable Development & Project Management*. Cologne: Lambert Academic Publishing.

Emmott, p. (2013). *Ten Billion*. London: Penguin.

Engel, B. (2011, February 20). Warum das Haus ein Auto braucht. *Welt am Sonntag, Beilage MOTOR*.

Franken, M. (2013). *Bericht aus der Zukunft*. München: oekom.

Frankfurter Allgemeine Zeitung. (2010, March 23). Abfallwirtschaft trägt zum Umweltschutz bei. *Frankfurter Allgemeine Zeitung*, p. T 6.

Frankfurter Allgemeine Zeitung. (2013, October 15). Krebs kostet 35 Milliarden Euro im Jahr. *Frankfurter Allgemeine Zeitung*, p. 18.

Gale, p. F. (2009a, November). Green Out. *PM Network*, pp. 40-45.

Gale, p. F. (2009b, December). The Real Deal. *PM Network*, pp. 30-35.

Global Footprint Network. (2013b, November 08). *Global Footprint Network Glossary.* Retrieved November 08, 2013, from Global Footprint Network: http://www.footprintnetwork.org/en/index.php/GFN/page/glossary/#biocapacity

Global Footprint Network. (2013b, November 08). *Global Footprint Network, Footprint Science, Data and Results.* Retrieved November 08, 2013, from Global Footprint Network: http://www.footprintnetwork.org/en/index.php/GFN/page/footprint_data_and_results/

Global Reporting Initiative (TM). (2013). *G4 Sustainability Reporting Guidelines.* Amsterdam: Global Reporting Initiative (TM).

Guarino, M. (2013, November). Weather Alert: Flooding Ahead. *PM Network*, pp. 48-55.

Hartmann, J., & Wüpper, G. (2011, June 21). Fliegen soll grüner werden. *Die Welt*, p. 6.

HAVI Logistics GmbH. (2010). *Umwelterklärung 2010-2012.* Duisburg: HAVI Logistics GmbH.

HM Government, UK. (2013). *The Companies Act 2006 (Strategic Report and Directors' Report) Regulations 2013.* Retrieved January 24, 2014, from legislation.gov.uk: http://www.legislation.gov.uk/ukdsi/2013/9780111540169/contents

Honest By. (2013, November 07). *honest by.* Retrieved November 07, 2013, from honest by: http://www.honestby.com/en/product/58/jackets/navy-blue-unisex-organic-denim-bomber-jacket-with-tweed-sleeves.html imug Beratungsgesellschaft für sozial-ökologische Innovationen mbH. (2013, November 12). *Nachhaltigkeitsratings: Unternehmen.* Retrieved November 13, 2013, from imug: http://www.imug. de/index.php/nachhaltiges-investment/ratings-unternehmen. html

IPCC. (2007a). *Contribution of Working Group I to the Fourth Assessment Report of the Intergovernmental Panel on Climate Change.* Cambridge, New York: Cambridge University Press.

IPCC. (2007b). *IPCC Fourth Assessment Report (AR4).* Retrieved November 14, 2013, from Intergovernmental Panel on Climate Change: http://www.ipcc.ch/publications_and_data/ publications_ipcc_fourth_assessment_report_wg1_report_ the_physical_science_basis.htm

Logicalis U.S. (2013). *IT Carbon & Power Consumption Calculator.* Retrieved November 18, 2013, from Logicalis: http://www. us.logicalis.com/tools/it-carbon--power-consumption.aspx

Maltzman, R., & Shirley, D. (2011). *Green Project Management.* Boca Raton: CRC Press.

McEachran, R. (2011). *New toolkit reveals natural capital costs.* Retrieved December 04, 2013, from greenfutures magazine: http://www.forumforthefuture.org/greenfutures/articles/new-toolkit-reveals-natural-capital-costs

Merschmann, H. (2008, März). Die Computer werden grün. *mobil,* pp. 36-40.

Microsoft Corp. (2009, Januar). *Berichte aus der Praxis: Was ist eigentlich grüne IT?* Retrieved November 15, 2013, from TechNet Magazine: http://technet.microsoft.com/de-de/magazine/2009.01.fieldnotes.aspx

Mrusek, K. (2007, December 17). Der Klima-Umbau. *Frankfurter Allgemeine Zeitung*, p. 1.

Planko, J., & Silvius, G. (2012). Sustainability in Business. In G. Silvius, R. Schipper, J. Planko, J. van den Brink, & A. Köhler, *Sustainability in Project Management* (pp. 7-20). Farnham: Gower Publishing Limited.

Project Management Institute. (2013a). *A Guide to the Project Management Body of Knowledge (PMBoK Guide) Fifth Edition*. Newtown Square: Project Management Institute, Inc.

Project Management Institute. (2013b). *The Standard for Program Management Third Edition*. Newtown Square: Project Management Institute, Inc.

Project Management Instiute Inc. (2007). *2008 Leadership in Project Management*. Newtown Square: Project Management Institute.

Sächsische Zeitung. (2013, June 13). 100 Millionen Euro Flutschaden erwartet. *Sächsische Zeitung*, p. 1.

Schrader, C. (2013, December 17). Klimawandel konkret. *Süddeutsche Zeitung*, p. 16.

Silvius, G., & Schipper, R. (2012). Sustainability and Projects. In G. Silvius, R. Schipper, J. Planko, J. van den Brink, & A. Köhler, *Sustainability in Project Management* (pp. 21-44). Farnham: Gower Publishing Limited.

Silvius, G., Schipper, R., Planko, J., van den Brink, J., & Köhler, A. (2012). *Sustainability in Project Management.* Farnham: Gower Publishing Limited.

Stadtwerke München GmbH. (2012). *SWM.* Retrieved November 19, 2013, from Informationen zu M-Strom: http://www.swm.de/privatkunden/m-strom/informationen.html

TechSoup Global. (2013). *Green Technology.* Retrieved November 15, 2013, from techsoup.org: http://www.techsoup.org/green-technology

The CarbonNeutral Company Limited. (2013a). *Mandatory Carbon Reporting.* Retrieved December 06, 2013, from The CarbonNeutral Company: http://www.carbonneutral.com/our-services/carbon-footprint-assessments/mandatory-carbon-reporting/

The CarbonNeutral Company Limited. (2013b). *Business carbon calculators.* Retrieved December 10, 2013, from The CarbonNeutral Company: http://www.carbonneutral.com/our-services/channel-partners/carbon-calculators/

Thema 1 GmbH. (2013, November 08). *Low Carbon Society.* Retrieved November 08, 2013, from CO_2 Fußabdruck: http://www.pcf-projekt.de/main/background/low-carbon-society/

Tomorrow's Company. (2013). *Tomorrow's Business Owners*. Retrieved December 05, 2013, from tomorrow's company: http://tomorrowscompany.com/tomorrows-business-owners

Toyota Deutschland GmbH. (2013, November 05). *Prius Plug-in Hybrid*. Retrieved November 05, 2013, from www.toyota.de: http://www.toyota.de/cars/new_cars/prius-plugin/index.tmex

U.S. Environmental Protection Agency. (2013). *Computers for Consumers*. Retrieved November 15, 2013, from Energy Star: http://www.energystar.gov/index.cfm?fuseaction=find_a_product.ShowProductGroup&pgw_code=CO

U.S. Green Building Council. (2013). *LEED v4*. Retrieved December 13, 2013, from Leadership in Energy & Environmental Design: http://www.usgbc.org/leed/v4

United Nations. (1987, December). *Report of the World Commission on Environment and Development*. Retrieved November 20, 2013, from UN Documents: http://www.un-documents.net/ocf-02.htm#I

University of Cambridge. (2013). *Natural Capital Leaders Platform*. Retrieved December 04, 2013, from University of Cambridge Programme for Sustainability: http://www.cpsl.cam.ac.uk/Business-Platforms/Natural-Capital-Leaders-Platform.aspx

University of Cambridge Programme for Sustainability Leadership. (2013). *The Cambridge Natural Capital Leaders Platform - E.Valu.TE: The Practical Guide*. Cambridge: University of Cambridge Programme for Sustainability Leadership.

Verkehrsclub Deutschland e.V. (2007, June). Gottfried Ilgmanns Zahlen. *fairkehr*, p. 27.

Wagner, R. (2012, August 6). *GPM Blog*. Retrieved September 26, 2013, from http://gpm-blog.de/iso-21500-guidance-on-project-management-nimmt-letzte-hurde/

Weindl, G. (2008, January 10). Einkehrschwung mit Emissionshandel. *Frankfurter Allgemeine Zeitung*, p. R1.

Wikipedia. (2013a, November 08). *Kamerun*. Retrieved November 08, 2013, from Wikipedia: http://de.wikipedia.org/wiki/Kamerun

Wikipedia. (2013b, November 12). *Heizwert*. Retrieved November 15, 2013, from Wikipedia: http://de.wikipedia.org/wiki/Heizwert#Feste_Brennstoffe_.28bei_25.C2.A0.C2.B0C.29

Wikipedia. (2013c, Ocotober). *City of New York*. Retrieved November 28, 2013, from Wikipedia: http://de.wikipedia.org/wiki/New_York_City#Bev.C3.B6lkerung

Wikipedia. (2013d, November 21). *Niederlande*. Retrieved November 28, 2013, from Wikipedia: http://de.wikipedia.org/wiki/Niederlande#Bev.C3.B6lkerung

Wikipedia. (2013e, December 03). *Wasserelektrolyse*. Retrieved December 13, 2013, from Wikipedia: http://de.wikipedia.org/wiki/Wasserelektrolyse

World Business Council for Sustainable Development. (2013).
WBCSD Tool Box. Retrieved December 13, 2013, from
WBCSD Business Solutions for a Sustainable World: http://
www.wbcsd.org/Pages/EDocument/EDocumentDetails.aspx?I
D=15700&NoSearchContextKey=true

World Resources Institute - WRI. (2009). *Sustainable Procurement
of Wood and Paper-based Products: Guide and resource
kit.* Washington: World Business Council for Sustainable
Development - WBCSD.

Ziener, M., & Rinke, A. (2009, Juni 29). Obamas Umweltgesetz wenig
geliebt. *Handelsblatt*, p. 5.

10   Index

II Abbreviations

3BL	Triple Bottom Line
BUWAL	Bundesamt für Umwelt, Wald und Landwirtschaft, Switzerland
cbm	Cubic Meters
CH_4	Methane
CO_2	Carbon dioxide
CO_2-EQ	Carbon dioxide equivalent
CoP	Community of Practice
CoQ	Cost of Quality
CSR	Corporate Social Responsibility
DEFRA	Department for Environment, Food and Rural Affairs
EBP	Environmental Burden Point
GFN	Global Footprint Network
gha	Global Hectares
GRI	Global Reporting Initiative
GWP	Global Warming Potential
HFCs	Hydrofluorocarbons
IPCC	Intergovernmental Panel on Climate Change
KPI	Key Performance Indicator
N_2O	Nitrous Oxide (laughing gas)
PFCs	Perfluorinated compounds
PMI®	Project Management Institute
ROI	Return on Investment
SCS	Sustainable Committed Sellers
SF_6	Sulfur hexafluoride
SMEs	Small and Medium Companies
t/a	tons per year

UK	United Kingdom
UN	United Nations
USGBC	U.S. Green Building Council

12 Picture Credits

Figure 1: Drought in Bavaria Summer 2013	Heinz Fabrinsky, 2013
Figure 2: New Orleans in the Floods of 2005	AP Photo/U.S. Coast Guard, Petty Officer 2nd Class Kyle Niemi. This image or file is the work of a United States Coast Guard service personnel or employee, taken or made as part of that person's official duties. As a work of the U.S. federal government, the image or file is in the public domain (17 U.S.C. § 101 and § 105, USCG main privacy policy and specific privacy policy for its imagery server)
About the Author	Thomas Friedemann, Dresden; © Heinz Fabrinsky

13   About the Author

Heinz Fabrinsky holds a diploma in economics and is a qualified banker. For almost 20 years he has been doing research on methods for ecological accounting of economic activities.

Research and working experiences in the deserts of Southern Africa and the Middle East have contributed to his knowledge about the extreme consequences human behavior can have on the environment.

He has been certified as a Project Management Professional (PMP®) for more than 10 years. As such he is working as a consultant and trainer in project management and as a certified consultant for data protection.

In 2013 he founded the nonprofit company "BibeZu Bildung für eine bessere Zukunft gemeinnützige GmbH" and is acting as general manager for this corporation. BibeZu aims at research and training for sustainable methods of working and living.

Three Steps to Sustainability summarizes his knowledge and experience of ecological accounting. He has developed a comprehensive framework for project managers, who are looking for applicable tools in order to make their projects a better contribution to the sustainable development of our global economy.

He lives in Dresden, Germany together with his family.